CRAVINGS

Cravings

COMFORT EATS AND FAVOURITE TREATS

DEBBIE HARDING

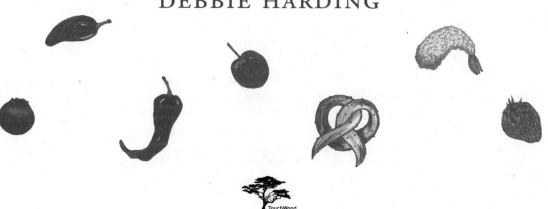

TouchWood
Editions

TouchWood Editions
www.touchwoodeditions.com

LIBRARY AND ARCHIVES CANADA CATALOGUING IN PUBLICATION
Harding, Debbie, 1956–
Cravings : comfort eats and favourite treats / Debbie Harding.

Includes index.
Issued also in electronic formats.
ISBN 978-1-926971-68-1

1. Cooking. 2. Cookbooks. I. Title.

TX714.H3647 2011   641.5   C2011-904161-8

Editor: Holland Gidney
Design: Pete Kohut
Cover and interior illustrations: Debbie Harding
Author photo: Doug Harding

BRITISH COLUMBIA ARTS COUNCIL
Supported by the Province of British Columbia

Canada Council for the Arts

Conseil des Arts du Canada

Canadian Heritage   Patrimoine canadien

We gratefully acknowledge the financial support for our publishing activities
from the Government of Canada through the Canada Book Fund, Canada
Council for the Arts, and the province of British Columbia through the
British Columbia Arts Council and the Book Publishing Tax Credit.

MIX
Paper from
responsible sources
FSC® C016245
FSC
www.fsc.org

The interior pages of this book have been printed on 100% post-consumer
recycled paper, processed chlorine free, and printed with vegetable-based inks.

The information in this book is true and complete to the best of the author's knowledge.
All recommendations are made without guarantee on the part of the author.
The author disclaims any liability in connection with the use of this information.

1 2 3 4 5 15 14 13 12 11

PRINTED IN CANADA

Cravings, my second cookbook, would not have been possible without the love and support of my family. So I would like to dedicate this book to all the members of my family, and my husband Doug's, to recognize each and every person's contribution. I am very happy and lucky to be a part of their lives.

A special dedication goes to my father, "Mac," for all his support and love over the years—through the good times and the difficult times. I wouldn't be the person I am today without his help, mentoring, and endless sense of humour.

To my sister, Brenda, for her amazing enthusiasm when *Go Nuts* was released and for her avid promotion of the same. Her love of new and interesting recipes helps to stimulate my creativity.

To my brother, Greg, for his entrepreneurial spirit—like me, inherited from Dad—and his never-ending excitement over new ways to cook fun foods.

Also to Wayne, Laura, Joel, Logan, and Ashley, my test kitchen audience and official tasters. I hope to expand this group to include Greg, Susan, Scott, and Dan on a regular basis when they make it out to the west coast.

And, as always and for always, to my husband, Doug, for being there for me everyday and loving me unconditionally. I love you all.

Table of Contents

viii   A Message from the Author

1   Breakfast & Brunch
17   Weekend Lunches
35   Small Bites
55   Casual Crowd Pleasers
85   Family Favourites
111   Showtime Snacks & Party Pleasers
133   Sweet Treats

156   Ingredient Reference List
      and Recommended Brands
158   Metric Conversion Chart
158   Standard Baking Pan Sizes
      and Capacity
159   Index
165   Acknowledgments

A Message from the Author

My family was lucky; we grew up with a mom who enjoyed cooking and who made family dinners each and every night. Sunday was always a big meal like roast beef with mashed potatoes and gravy, or roast chicken. Monday to Thursday, she cooked tasty traditional dinners like stew, cutlets, chops, tuna casserole, chili, potpies, and meatloaf.

But Friday and Saturday, it was fun food like baked spaghetti with meat sauce, homemade mac and cheese, or fried chicken. *Yum!* In the summer, there were barbecued burgers, ribs, or steak with potato salad. In the winter, we snacked on "nuts and bolts," and enjoyed homemade pizza and seafood chowder. My parents had a big deep fryer (quite a luxury in the sixties) so Mom sometimes even made us fish and chips, egg rolls, and donuts. We were in heaven! Weekend meals and snacks were definitely our favourites; they were put on this earth to satisfy our cravings for things that were salty, spicy, crispy, or sweet.

Some of these foods came to be associated with particular activities. For instance, hot chocolate with mini marshmallows after skiing and homemade ice cream on hot summer days at our cabin. *Huckleberry Hound* cartoons bring back memories of homemade cinnamon buns and fresh donuts; movies and TV specials induce cravings for popcorn, chips, and nuts.

Inevitably, enjoying these treats led to the development of specific food cravings among each and every family member. Whenever we were craving something, we would mention it to Mom and secretly hope it would magically appear over the following few days.

When I was growing up, my father would often roam around the kitchen saying, "I feel like something . . ." followed by, "What do I want?" and then, inevitably, "How about some cheese and crackers?" Of course, it was not just any cheese; it had to be aged or sharp cheddar. (Though sometimes he would open a can of smoked oysters and serve them on crackers with small dollops of ketchup and HP sauce—on a special occasion, no doubt.) My brother soon followed suit. Like father, like son, I guess, except Greg's version of cheese and crackers was nachos laden with cheddar cheese and piled high with every imaginable topping. My mom and sister usually had the breakfast and baking cravings: Brenda loved waffles and Mom would choose something like lemon meringue pie. Amusingly, my husband, Doug, has picked up my dad's habit of asking, "What should I have?" But his answer usually involves dark chocolate, or when it's salt he's craving, chips or nuts appear.

Many cravings have nostalgic roots. One of my favourite treats as a child was celery sticks with Cheez

Whiz on them. They were crunchy *and* salty so they satisfied two food desires. I suppose Mom and Dad were just happy to see that their kids were eating some form of vegetable as a snack. Or perhaps one of them introduced the snack to us because of one of their own cravings; we all crave different things.

Doug and I decided some time ago that we should eat healthy during the week. This means low-fat dinners with lots of vegetables, lean meats and fish, and avoiding processed foods and desserts (although dark chocolate is still a must). But we don't worry about our diet as much on the weekends. It makes sense to us because it can be more difficult to make healthy choices when you are going out to restaurants or joining family and friends for meals. We also have one night each week when we can eat anything we want, which could be homemade French fries, chicken wings, or spring rolls. We call that day "Fryday" and, interestingly enough, it usually does occur on Friday. Some of the recipes in this book are quite indulgent and should only be reserved for "Frydays" but I believe we should all be able to enjoy fun foods without feeling guilty about it. Even the most strict weight-loss diets let you have a free day or "extra points" for a once-a-week treat.

One of the reasons I wrote this book was so people could satisfy their food cravings at home. I think it is very important to know what you are consuming, which is not always possible at fast food restaurants. If you cook your own food, though, you can control the amount of sugar and salt, and the type of fat (good or bad) and protein used. And it is easier to eliminate preservatives and additives if you read labels and choose your ingredients well. My Grilled Chicken Poutine (p. 62) is made with fat-free gravy and oven fries; a healthier version than takeout but still delicious. Another reason to cook these fun foods yourself is that you can control the portion size and enjoy treats appropriate to your appetite or diet restrictions. You may want a large portion if you just ran a marathon or did a hard workout; you may want a half portion if you are trying to limit calories or only want a snack.

I encourage you to indulge responsibly but still enjoy life's little pleasures without worry or stress. We all deserve rewards for our hard work (or workout). And when there is a cause for celebration, we should be able to participate in the festivities without guilt. Many of the tasty treats in this book have cured cravings for my family and circle of friends so I hope you will put them to the test against your powerful cravings and I hope you have fun trying them out.

Crave on!

—Debbie Harding

Breakfast & Brunch

2   Honey Cinnamon Buns

5   Ham and Cheese
Breakfast Buns

6   Breakfast Baguette
Sandwiches

7   Breakfast Burrito for One

8   Sunshine French Toast

9   Banana Chocolate Chip
Pancakes

10   Strawberry Cream Waffles

12   Baked Blueberry and
Brie Bread Pudding

13   Baked Eggs Ranchero Style

14   Heavenly Hash

15   Mexican Eggs Benedict

16   Quick Quiche

Honey Cinnamon Buns

A fabulous choice for Sunday morning and my brother Greg's favourite. When travelling, he searches high and low to find the best place to buy cinnamon buns; except when he comes to visit me. Of course, I can't resist adding nuts to the sauce but you can substitute raisins or omit them if that's your preference. A stand mixer is needed, or strong muscles, for kneading.

⅓ cup (80 mL) lukewarm water

¾ tsp (4 mL) white sugar for activating yeast

8 g package or 2¼ tsp (11 mL) regular (traditional) yeast

1½ cups (375 mL) hot water

1⅛ tsp (5.05 mL) salt

3 Tbsp plus 1 tsp (50 mL) canola or corn oil

5¾ to 6 cups (1.435 to 1.5 L) flour

3 Tbsp plus 1 tsp (50 mL) white sugar

1 to 2 tsp (5 to 10 mL) vegetable oil for bowl and baking pan

Makes 12 cinnamon buns for some very lucky people.

Per cinnamon bun (with pecans): 478 cals, 18.5 g fat, 6.7 g sat. fat, 26 mg cholesterol, 229 mg sodium, 70.8 g carbs, 7.1 g protein

Place lukewarm water in a medium bowl; add ¾ teaspoon (4 mL) sugar and stir to dissolve. Add yeast and whisk to combine. Let stand for 15 minutes to activate yeast; it will expand in volume and become a beige, foamy mixture.

While yeast is proofing, whisk together by hand hot water, 3 tablespoons plus 1 teaspoon (50 mL) sugar, and salt in a large mixing bowl, or stand mixer bowl. Add oil and let cool to room temperature. When mixing bowl contents are lukewarm, add yeast mixture. If mixture is too hot, yeast may not work as well; if it is too cold, dough will not rise as quickly. Stir mixtures together until incorporated, then add 4 cups (1 L) flour and stir with a wooden spoon. Dough will be sloppy and appear lumpy.

If using a stand mixer, place bowl on mixer stand and insert dough hook attachment. Mix on medium-low speed for 30 seconds to smooth dough. Drop speed to lowest setting and gradually add remaining flour. Add only about 2 tablespoons (30 mL) flour at a time or the flour may come back at you. Continue until you have ¼ cup (60 mL) to go. Mixing can also be done by hand; just keep kneading continuously. This step will take about 10 minutes.

Feel dough with your fingers. It should be soft and smooth—not too sticky. If dough is still sticky, add remaining flour gradually.

Dough should pull away from the sides of the bowl when ready. Remove dough from bowl and scrape the sides. On a clean surface, knead dough by hand for a few seconds to smooth it and form a ball. Add a sprinkle of flour if dough sticks.

Oil a medium-large bowl and place dough in it; turn over once to coat with oil. Cover with a clean tea towel or plastic wrap. Let rise in a warm, draft-free area for 1 hour, or until doubled in volume.

While dough is rising, make the Honey-Cinnamon Sauce. Lightly oil a 9 × 13 × 2 inch (23 × 33 × 5 cm) baking pan. In a medium bowl, combine honey, butter, brown sugar, and cinnamon; mix well with a spoon. Crush any sugar lumps in the mixture, then add nuts or raisins (if using). Add mixture to baking pan, distributing sauce evenly over the bottom with a spreader knife or spatula. (It is customary to taste sauce remaining on the spoon—just to see if it is satisfactory, of course!) Set pan aside until dough is ready.

When dough has doubled, press it down using your fist to expel all the air; do this all over the dough. Remove dough from the bowl, and press or roll out on a clean surface to form a rectangle measuring 16 × 14 inches (40 × 35 cm). Don't flour the board or counter because you want the dough to stick to the surface and hold in place.

Avoiding the top inch (2.5 cm) and bottom edge, spread dough evenly with soft butter. Sprinkle the buttered area evenly with brown sugar and cinnamon. Roll the rectangle up tightly to make a 16-inch (40 cm) log and seal up the ends. Lifting both ends of the log, gently stretch until 18 inches (45 cm) long and 2½ inches (6 cm) wide; the log should be even and smooth.

With a sharp knife, cut the log into two 9-inch (23 cm) pieces, then cut each half in two. Finally, cut each of the four lengths into three pieces. You should have 12 pieces, each about 1¼ inch (3 cm) wide.

Honey-Cinnamon Sauce
⅓ cup (80 mL) honey
3 Tbsp (45 mL) melted butter
⅔ cup (160 mL) brown sugar
2 tsp (10 mL) cinnamon
⅔ cup (160 mL) toasted pecans, chopped, or raisins

Cinnamon Bun Filling
¼ cup plus 3 Tbsp (105 mL) butter, softened
¾ cup (185 mL) brown sugar
1 Tbsp (15 mL) cinnamon

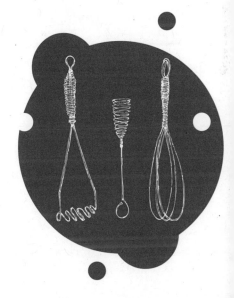

Placing each slice flat in the pan (so spiral rings are visible), make four rows of three slices. Cover buns with a clean tea towel and let rise for 1 hour, or until doubled and risen above pan edge by about ½ inch (1 cm). When buns have risen about three-quarters of the way, preheat the oven to 400°F (200°C).

Bake buns in bottom third of the oven for 25 minutes. Check after 20 minutes; if tops are already dark golden brown on top, drop temperature to 375°F (190°C) for final 5 minutes. Remove buns from the oven and test for doneness by knocking on tops of buns with your knuckles. They should sound hollow—if they don't, cook for 5 more minutes. When done, let cool for 5 minutes.

Place a baking sheet over buns and, using oven mitts, invert pan onto tray securely and then place on a cooling rack. Still wearing oven mitts, remove top pan. Scrape out any remaining sauce and spread overtop buns. Do the same with any sauce that runs down onto the baking sheet. Be careful: the sugar is extremely hot when it comes out of the oven. Sauce will thicken up as it cools.

Ham and Cheese Breakfast Buns

These buns are a great side with eggs, or as portable breakfast for on-the-go individuals. If desired, you can substitute Italian prosciutto for the Black Forest ham.

Follow dough instructions as for Cinnamon Buns (p. 2). Press or roll out dough to make a rectangle measuring 16 × 14 inches (40 × 35 cm).

Instead of a sweet filling, spread dough with Dijon mustard. Top with ham slices, trimming to fit if needed, and cheese. Carefully and tightly roll up the rectangle to make a log. Seal up the ends, and then cut into 12 equal slices with a very sharp, non-serrated knife.

Lightly oil a 9 × 13 × 2 inch (23 × 33 × 5 cm) baking pan. Placing each slice flat in the pan (so spiral rings are visible), make 4 rows of 3 slices. Cover buns with a clean tea towel and let rise for 1 hour, or until they have doubled and risen above pan edge by about ½ inch (1 cm). When buns have risen about three-quarters of the way, preheat the oven to 400°F (200°C).

Bake buns in bottom third of the oven for 25 minutes. Check after 20 minutes; if tops are already dark golden brown on top, drop temperature to 375°F (190°C) for final 5 minutes. Remove buns from oven and test for doneness by knocking on tops of buns with your knuckles. They should sound hollow—if they don't, cook for 5 more minutes. When done, let buns rest in the pan for 5 to 10 minutes before turning them out onto a rack to cool and then pulling them apart.

Dough

1 recipe dough from Honey Cinnamon Buns (p. 2)

1 to 2 tsp (5 to 10 mL) vegetable oil for bowl and baking pan

Filling

⅓ cup (80 mL) Dijon mustard

8 large, thin slices Black Forest ham, about 8 oz (250 g)

1½ cups (375 mL) grated sharp or aged cheddar cheese

Makes 12 medium buns.

Per bun: 367 cals, 12 g fat, 4.3 g sat. fat, 28 mg cholesterol, 739 mg sodium, 49.8 g carbs, 15.1 g protein

Breakfast Baguette Sandwiches

Here's an excellent prep-ahead breakfast sandwich that you can finish in the oven, on the barbecue, or over the campfire (if you dare). You can substitute 1 cup (250 mL) diced ham for the bacon, or use ½ cup (125 mL) diced roasted red pepper for a vegetarian version.

vegetable oil for skillet

8 large eggs, beaten

½ tsp (2 mL) salt

¼ tsp (1 mL) pepper

1 cup (250 mL) grated aged or sharp cheddar cheese, divided

8 slices side bacon, cooked crisp, drained, and chopped into ½-inch (1 cm) pieces

8 medium mushrooms, sliced and cooked in 1 to 2 tsp (5 to 10 mL) olive oil until light golden

1 French baguette, 18 × 3 inches (45 × 8 cm)

heavy-duty aluminum foil

Serves 4.

Per serving: 740 cals, 43.2 g fat, 17.3 g sat. fat, 488 mg cholesterol, 1747 mg sodium, 47.3 g carbs, 40.2 g protein

Cooking Tip: Preheating the skillet on high heat prevents the egg from coating it with a film of egg, and makes it easier to clean afterwards.

In a medium-large bowl, whisk eggs with salt and pepper until yolks and seasoning are incorporated. Preheat a large, oiled non-stick skillet on high heat until hot, about 1 to 2 minutes. Add eggs and cook, stirring with a wooden spoon or heatproof spatula, for about 1 minute. Lift any cooked egg from the bottom of the pan and mix it in with remaining liquid egg. Repeat until eggs are completely set, about 3 to 4 minutes. Reduce the heat to medium-high if eggs are cooking too quickly or browning. You want scrambled eggs that are set but not browned.

With a bread knife, slice open the baguette lengthwise, leaving one side uncut to create a hinge. With your fingers, remove the inside bread from each half to create 2 shallow troughs 2 inches (5 cm) wide and 1 inch (2.5 cm) deep. Sprinkle ½ cup (125 mL) cheddar into each trough. Add mushrooms to bottom half and top with scrambled eggs, spreading them out evenly and then gently pressing down. Add bacon pieces to top half, then quickly press baguette closed.

Place baguette lengthwise on a sheet of heavy-duty aluminum foil at least 24 inches (60 cm) long. Wrap baguette tightly in foil. Refrigerate with seam side up for up to 1 day prior to baking.

About 30 minutes prior to baking, remove wrapped loaf from the fridge and preheat the oven to 375°F (190°C). Bake foil-wrapped loaf for 20 minutes, or until heated through. Remove foil, cut into 4 pieces, and serve.

Breakfast Burrito for One

Another great on-the-go breakfast. Make a bunch one to two days ahead for a filling meal that is quick to heat up and eat, or easy to wrap to take with you. Ingredients given are for one burrito; to make more, multiply the quantities accordingly.

In a medium-large bowl, whisk eggs, then add chilies and seasoning; mix well. Heat a medium, oiled non-stick skillet on medium-high heat until hot, about 2 to 3 minutes. Add egg mixture and scramble eggs until just set, about 2 to 3 minutes. Remove from heat and ready remaining burrito ingredients.

Place tortilla on a microwavable dinner plate and cover with waxed paper or a specially designed cover to prevent it from drying out. Heat for 15 seconds (per tortilla) on medium heat. (Warming tortillas makes them more pliable for folding and less likely to break. But they only stay warm and pliable for a few minutes so only heat as needed.)

Add eggs to bottom third of tortilla and spread out until about 4 inches (10 cm) long and 2 inches (5 cm) wide. Distribute salsa along top edge of eggs, topping with ¼ cup (60 mL) cheese.

To roll, curl lower edge of tortilla up over filling. Next, fold in each side of tortilla, and hold them in as you roll up the burrito. Place burrito seam side down on a plate for heating in the microwave, or store in an airtight container in the fridge until later.

Just before heating, top burrito with ¼ cup (60 mL) cheddar, then microwave uncovered on medium-high heat, or 75% power, for 3 minutes, or until heated through. Cheese should be melted and burrito will have puffed up. Serve with additional salsa on the side, if desired.

vegetable oil for skillet

2 large eggs, beaten

1½ tsp (7 mL) chopped, rinsed, and drained canned mild green chilies (see Cooking Tip)

⅛ tsp (0.5 mL) salt

⅛ tsp (0.5 mL) pepper

10-inch (25 cm) flour tortilla, preferably Olafson's brand

2 Tbsp (30 mL) thick medium salsa

½ cup (125 mL) grated sharp or aged cheddar cheese, divided

Makes 1 burrito.

Per burrito: 538 cals, 34.9 g fat, 18 g sat. fat, 491 mg cholesterol, 1284 mg sodium, 23.9 g carbs, 32.1 g protein

Cooking Tip: When using canned green chilies, rinse and drain them well. Use the portion that you need, then freeze the rest in an airtight container for up to 3 months. One 4-oz (125 mL) can yields about 24 tsp of chilies, or enough for 18 burritos.

Tortillas usually have one good side, which is smooth and free of any circles or bubbles, while the other side is less attractive due to flattened bubbles and creases. Heat the tortilla with the blemished side up on the plate so it ends up on the inside of the burrito.

Sunshine French Toast

Orange, vanilla, and cinnamon—the flavours in this recipe are one of my favourite combinations. I chose Sunshine for the name because it shines!

2 large eggs
⅔ cup (160 mL) light cream or whole milk
1 tsp (5 mL) brandy or orange-flavoured brandy
½ tsp (2 mL) vanilla
2 Tbsp (30 mL) sugar
¼ tsp (1 mL) cinnamon
1 tsp (5 mL) orange zest
6 slices thick-sliced white or brown bread
½ cup (125 mL) canola oil for frying
1 cup (250 mL) warm maple syrup for serving

Per half slice with 2 Tbsp (30 mL) syrup:
195 cals, 5.3 g fat, 2.8 g sat. fat,
57 mg cholesterol, 133 mg sodium,
33.5 g carbs, 3.4 g protein

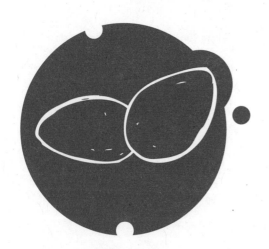

Preheat the oven to 250°F (120°C). In a medium bowl, beat eggs with a whisk. Add cream, brandy, vanilla, sugar, and cinnamon; whisk to dissolve sugar. Add zest, stir to combine, and set aside.

Preheat oil in a large non-stick skillet on medium-high for 2 to 3 minutes. Oil should be rippling but not smoking. Dip both sides of bread slices in egg mixture; coat completely but do not soak thoroughly. Prepare slices one at a time, letting any excess liquid run back into the bowl.

Place 2 to 3 dipped slices in hot oil, depending on how many will fit in the pan. Fry each side to golden brown, about 2 to 3 minutes per side, using tongs or a lifter to flip slices as they brown. When both sides are browned, remove slices and drain on paper towels. Keep warm in the oven in a baking dish. Repeat frying process until all slices are browned, then slice pieces of French toast in half diagonally. Serve 3 halves per person with syrup on the side.

Zesting Citrus Fruits: Wash and dry the citrus fruit. Over a medium bowl, hold the fruit in your left hand and the zester in your right hand (or vice-versa if you are left-handed). Remove the peel (coloured part) in short downward motions, continuing until the fruit is almost completely white. Freeze any extra zest in an airtight container or bag for later use. Afterwards, cut the white pith off the zested fruit from top to bottom, trimming right down to the flesh, then cut the fruit crosswise to make slices to garnish food or beverages. Purchase seedless fruit such as navel oranges for a nicer presentation and easier preparation.

Banana Chocolate Chip Pancakes

My maternal grandfather, Grandpa Poole, always made us animal-shaped pancakes: bunny rabbits, bears, and maybe the odd kitty cat (see Shaping Pancakes). The batter was plain but the presentation sure wasn't to his grandkids. I can't imagine how thrilled we would have been with banana chocolate chip bears!

Preheat the oven to 250°F (120°C) to keep pancakes warm. In a large bowl, place all the dry ingredients except chocolate chips and whisk to blend. Stir in chocolate chips and set aside. In a medium bowl, whisk eggs together, then add buttermilk and vanilla, whisking to blend. Add banana and butter; mix well. Make a well in the dry ingredients and pour in the liquid. Stir until just combined; the mixture will be thick.

Heat 1 to 1½ teaspoons (5 to 7.5 mL) oil in a large non-stick skillet or a griddle on medium-high heat for 1 to 2 minutes until pan is hot. One at a time, add ¼ cup (60 mL) portions of batter, spreading out the batter to form 4-inch (10 cm) circles. Fry in batches of 3 or 4 at a time; don't crowd them.

Fry pancakes for about 2 minutes, or until golden and the bubbles have popped, then flip over and brown the other side for 1 to 2 minutes more. Place on a baking tray and keep warm in the oven. Repeat the process until all the pancakes are cooked.

Shaping Pancakes: Animal-shaped pancakes are fun to make for little (or big) kids.
For a bear, make a circle of batter 3 inches (5 cm) across for the body, then add a second 1½-inch (4 cm) circle of batter at 12 o'clock for the head and drop 4 tiny dots of batter touching the edges of the 3-inch (5 cm) circle at 2, 4, 8, and 10 o'clock for paws. Add round ears to the head with drops of batter at 10 o'clock and 2 o'clock.

1½ cups (375 mL) flour

3 Tbsp (45 mL) sugar

1½ tsp (7 mL) baking powder

½ tsp (2 mL) baking soda

¼ tsp (1 mL) salt

2 large eggs

1½ cups (375 mL) buttermilk (shake well before measuring)

2 Tbsp (30 mL) melted butter

1 tsp (5 mL) vanilla

1 large ripe banana, puréed (about ½ to ⅔ cup [125 to 160 mL])

½ cup (125 mL) chocolate chips

1 Tbsp (15 mL) canola oil for frying

1 cup (250 mL) warm maple syrup for serving

Makes 16 pancakes.

Per pancake with 1 Tbsp (15 mL) syrup: 189 cals, 5.1 g fat, 2.9 g sat. fat, 33 g cholesterol, 110 mg sodium, 32.4 g carbs, 3.4 g protein

Strawberry Cream Waffles

Sounds like a birthday or Valentine's Day breakfast to me! You'll need a waffle iron for this one, or substitute purchased waffles if you must.

Strawberry Sauce

Strawberry Sauce

1 lb (500 g) unsweetened frozen strawberries, thawed

1 cup (250 mL) icing sugar, sifted after measuring

1 Tbsp (15 mL) lemon juice

1 Tbsp (15 mL) brandy

1 pint (500 mL) fresh strawberries, hulled and sliced ½ inch (1 cm) thick

In a food processor, purée thawed berries and strain them to yield about 1 cup (250 mL) purée. Gradually whisk in icing sugar, then lemon juice and brandy; whisk until smooth. You can make the sauce 1 to 2 days ahead, cover and refrigerate or freeze the sauce in an airtight container for up to 3 months. Add fresh, sliced berries just before serving.

Makes 4 cups (1 L).

Chantilly Cream

Chantilly Cream

1 cup (250 mL) whipping cream

3 Tbsp (45 mL) icing sugar

¼ tsp (1 mL) vanilla

Per waffle with ½ cup (125 mL) sauce and ¼ cup (60 mL) cream: 406 cals, 20 g fat, 11.9 g sat. fat, 116 mg cholesterol, 200 mg sodium, 50.2 g carbs, 6.5 g protein

Using a hand-held mixer (or a stand mixer), whip cream in a deep medium bowl on high speed until soft peaks form, about 3 to 4 minutes. Scrape down the sides of the bowl with a spatula and whip cream for another 1 to 2 minutes, until firm peaks appear. Cover and refrigerate until ready to assemble waffles.

Makes 2 cups (500 mL).

Waffles

Preheat waffle iron according to the manufacturer's instructions. Preheat the oven to 250°F (120°C) for keeping cooked waffles warm. In a large bowl, mix dry ingredients together, and then make a well in the ingredients. In a medium bowl, stir beaten eggs together with milk and melted butter, then pour into the well and mix only until smooth.

Referring to manufacturer's instructions, add recommended amount of batter to the waffle iron and close lid to cook. Cook waffles until steam stops escaping, and waffles are brown and crisp. Keep waffles warm in the oven until all the batter is used up.

Makes 8 four-inch (10 cm) waffles if using a standard waffle iron.

To assemble, top each waffle with ½ cup (125 mL) Strawberry Sauce and finish with ¼ cup (60 mL) Chantilly Cream.

Waffles

1½ cups (375 mL) flour
2 Tbsp (30 mL) sugar
1 Tbsp (15 mL) baking powder
½ tsp (2 mL) salt .
2 large eggs, beaten
1½ cups (375 mL) milk
¼ cup (60 mL) melted butter

Baked Blueberry and Brie Bread Pudding

A breakfast or brunch buffet dish extraordinaire! This recipe takes some time to prep but can be made 1 to 2 days ahead, which saves you a lot of time when you have guests.

Lightly oil a 9 × 13 inch (23 × 33 cm) baking dish. Slice bread ½ inch (1 cm) thick and line bottom of pan completely with approximately half the slices. Thinly slice rind off cheese, trying not to waste any of the cheese itself; discard rind. (It is okay if there are small bits of rind remaining on the cheese.) Slice cheese ¼ inch (6 mm) thick and cut slices into ½-inch (1 cm) cubes; evenly distribute them overtop the bread in the pan. Top cheese with blueberries, followed by another layer of bread slices.

In a large bowl, whisk eggs with sugar, salt, milk, and cinnamon. Pour mixture evenly overtop bread slices, then cover and refrigerate while it is absorbed. This step will take 1 to 2 hours but can be done up to 2 days ahead.

Remove the dish from the fridge 30 to 45 minutes before baking. Preheat the oven to 350°F (180°C) 10 minutes before baking.

Sprinkle bread pudding with cinnamon-sugar mixture and bake for 45 minutes, until puffed and golden. Serve with blueberry syrup on the side.

vegetable oil for baking dish

unsliced loaf Challah bread, or white bread with crusts removed

8 oz (250 g) Brie cheese

1½ cups (375 mL) fresh blueberries, or frozen ones, thawed and drained

6 large eggs, at room temperature

½ cup sugar (155 mL)

¼ tsp (1 mL) salt

2 cups (500 mL) whole milk or light cream

½ tsp (2 mL) cinnamon

2 Tbsp (30 mL) sugar mixed with ¼ tsp (1 mL) cinnamon for topping

blueberry syrup, or maple syrup

Makes twelve 3 × 4-inch (8 × 10 cm) portions.

Per serving (without syrup): 287 cals, 11.3 g fat, 6 g sat. fat, 148 mg cholesterol, 360 mg sodium, 35.1 g carbs, 11.1 g protein

Baked Eggs Ranchero Style

Spicy eggs for a fabulous weekend breakfast or brunch! Garnish them with a few tortilla chips for a little Mexican flair.

Preheat the oven to 375°F (190°C) and oil four 8-ounce (250 mL) ramekins.

In a large bowl, beat eggs with ¼ cup (60 mL) water and seasoning. Preheat a large, oiled non-stick skillet on medium-high for 2 to 3 minutes before adding egg mixture. Stirring almost continuously with a wooden spoon or heatproof spatula, cook eggs only until they are semi-solid, just 2 to 3 minutes. Eggs should be quite wet and loose, not fully set, as they will finish cooking in the oven.

Divide half the egg mixture among the 4 ramekins. Add 2 tablespoons (30 mL) salsa to each ramekin and spread it over the eggs; top with 2 tablespoons (30 mL) cheddar. Portion out remaining egg mixture among the ramekins. Top each dish with 2 tablespoons (30 mL) cheese and sprinkle with parsley or paprika to add some colour. You can prepare the omelettes ahead to this point; cover and refrigerate for up to 1 day.

Remove ramekins from the fridge 30 minutes before baking. Place on a baking sheet or in a shallow pan. Bake omelettes in lower third of the oven for 10 to 15 minutes, until cheese is bubbling and eggs are set. Serve remaining salsa on the side.

Omelettes

1 to 2 Tbsp (15 to 30 mL) vegetable oil for the skillet and ramekins

12 large eggs

½ tsp (2 mL) salt

½ tsp (2 mL) pepper

Filling

1 cup (250 mL) thick salsa, mild or medium

1 cup (250 mL) grated aged or sharp cheddar cheese

1 tsp (5 mL) dried parsley or ½ tsp (2 mL) paprika for garnish

Serves 4.

Per serving: 359 cals, 25.9 g fat, 11.6 g sat. fat, 666 mg cholesterol, 846 mg sodium, 4.1 g carbs, 27.2 g protein

Heavenly Hash

The potato mixture makes a delicious base for eggs; it also works as a fabulous side dish for entrées! The recipe can be easily doubled or tripled. You will be asked to make this one time and time again! This is Doug's and my favourite breakfast of all time!

1 cup (250 mL) cooked grated potato (see Preparing Grated Potato)

2 Tbsp (30 mL) finely chopped green onion, about 1 medium green onion

2 Tbsp (30 mL) finely chopped roasted red pepper

⅓ cup (80 mL) grated Asiago or Pecorino cheese

¼ tsp (1 mL) salt

¼ tsp (1 mL) pepper

1 Tbsp (15 mL) fresh parsley leaves, minced

2 Tbsp (30 mL) butter, divided

vegetable oil

2 large eggs, cold

⅛ tsp (0.5 mL) freshly ground coarse sea salt or Fleur de Sel

⅛ tsp (0.5 mL) freshly ground pepper

Serves 2.

Per serving: 363 cals, 24.3 g fat, 13.1 g sat. fat, 266 mg cholesterol, 604 mg sodium, 20.6 g carbs, 15.5 g protein

Preparing Grated Potato: Scrub and dry a medium-large unpeeled Russet potato. Poke with a fork several times and bake at 400°F (200°C) for 1 hour, or until tender throughout. Cool, remove the skin, and grate. Makes approximately 1 cup (250 mL).

Preheat the oven to 150°F (65°C) to keep potatoes warm while eggs cook.

In a medium bowl, stir together the first 7 ingredients. In a medium non-stick skillet, melt 1 tablespoon (15 mL) butter on medium-high heat until bubbling. Add potato mixture and divide into 2 equal portions. Press each one into a 3 × 4-inch (8 × 10 cm) oval, about ½ inch (1 cm) thick.

Cook patties until very golden on the bottom before turning them, about 4 to 5 minutes. (The cheese melts to holds them together.) When they are ready to be flipped, lift each one gently, slipping 1½ teaspoons (7.5 mL) butter under each patty as you turn it. Cook until patties are golden on both sides and cheese is melted. Set aside in the oven to keep warm while you prepare the eggs.

Heat a small non-stick skillet on high for 2 to 3 minutes until very hot. Coat the bottom with a thin coating of vegetable oil. Crack eggs into the pan, spacing them 1 inch (2.5 cm) apart; cook for 1 minute. Add 2 tablespoons (30 mL) water, which will spit and sputter, and immediately cover the pan with a lid. Turn off the heat but leave eggs on the burner, covered. Let stand for 1 minute to cook the egg whites while leaving the yolks soft, then remove from heat. If you like your yolks firmer, cook 30 to 60 seconds more.

Plate potato patties and top each one with an egg; sprinkle eggs with coarse salt and pepper.

Mexican Eggs Benedict

This recipe changes everything; a brave new twist for Eggs Benedict fans!

Set aside a bowl of ice water. Bring a large pot of water to a boil on high and add vinegar. Reduce the heat to a simmer so it's not quite boiling. One at a time, crack each egg into a small bowl or cup and then slide it into the water. Poach eggs until whites are set. Use a slotted spoon to transfer eggs to the bowl of ice water, which will stop the cooking, rinse off the vinegar, and chill them.

Cut bacon slices in half. Place English muffins on a baking sheet and preheat the oven broiler to 500°F (260°C) for toasting them. Put muffins under the broiler for 2 to 3 minutes (60 to 90 seconds per side) to crisp and lightly brown them. Turn the oven down to 175°F (80°C). Top each muffin half with 2 pieces of bacon and keep warm in the oven while you reheat the eggs.

Bring a large pot of water to a boil on high. Place eggs in the boiling water for 1 minute to reheat them, then remove one at a time using a slotted spoon. Drain eggs well, then add 1 egg to each prepared English muffin half. Top each "Benny" with 2 tablespoons (30 mL) warm Chili Con Queso and serve immediately.

1 Tbsp (15 mL) vinegar

8 large eggs, cold

8 slices side bacon, cooked crisp, drained on paper towels, and kept warm

4 English muffins, split into halves

2 cups (500 mL) Chili Con Queso (p. 125), warmed on low heat

Makes 8 "Bennies."

Per Benny: 341 cals, 22.3 g fat, 10.9 g sat. fat, 262 mg cholesterol, 1332 mg sodium, 13.7 g carbs, 21.3 g protein

Cooking Tip: To create round-shaped eggs, poach or fry them in a non-stick skillet in egg rings.

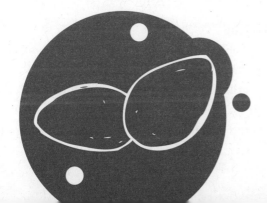

Quick Quiche

So that brunch is a breeze, prepare the quiche components the day before. Add a Caesar Salad and you are good to go.

9-inch (23 cm) unbaked deep-dish pie crust
4 large eggs
1 cup (250 mL) light cream
2 Tbsp (30 mL) minced fresh parsley leaves
1 recipe filling of your choice (see suggestions)
½ tsp (2 mL) salt
¼ tsp (1 mL) pepper
¼ tsp (1 mL) paprika
⅛ tsp (0.5 mL) cayenne powder
⅛ tsp (0.5 mL) ground nutmeg
1½ cups (375 mL) grated Edam, Monterey Jack, or Swiss cheese

Makes 8 lunch servings.

Per serving Seafood Quiche: 339 cals, 22.2 g fat, 9.5 g sat. fat, 225 mg cholesterol, 455 mg sodium, 12.9 g carbs, 22.2 g protein

Per serving Quiche Lorraine: 405 cals, 31.6 g fat, 13.1 g sat. fat, 158 mg cholesterol, 709 mg sodium, 13 g carbs, 17.2 g protein

Per serving Grilled Vegetable Quiche made using asparagus, grilled red peppers and mushrooms, ¾ cup (185 mL) each: 341 cals, 25.2 g fat, 12.1 g sat. fat, 157 mg cholesterol, 649 mg sodium, 14.5 g carbs, 14 g protein

Preheat the oven to 400°F (200°C). In a medium-large bowl, beat eggs; add cream and whisk until smooth. In a large bowl, toss filling gently with parsley, seasonings, and cheese. Add seasoned filling to pie crust and pour egg mixture slowly overtop. Crust should be three-quarters full; don't overfill.

Bake for 45 minutes, or until quiche centre is set and top is golden brown. The centre should not jiggle—it should be firm when tapped. Cool on a rack and let stand for 15 minutes before cutting.

Seafood Quiche

An elegant choice for brunch, and a favourite on both coasts. For the filling, use 1 lb (500 g) shelled, cooked seafood such as shrimp, crab or lobster meat (or a mix) and 1 bunch green onions, about 8 to 10, trimmed and sliced thinly.

Quiche Lorraine

This is a true classic and makes a perfect introduction to quiche. For the filling, use ¾ cup (185 mL) crisp-cooked side bacon (about 12 slices) or substitute diced cooked lean ham and ⅓ cup (80 mL) cooked diced onion, about half of a medium onion.

Grilled Vegetable Quiche

Grilled or roasted vegetables work equally well in this one so you can prepare it year-round. For the filling, use 2¼ cups (560 mL) chopped-up leftover grilled or oven-roasted vegetables, such as asparagus, sweet peppers, zucchini, mushrooms, eggplant, or onions, and 1 cup (250 mL) crumbled feta cheese, rinsed and drained well.

Weekend Lunches

Salads

18 Classic Caesar Salad with Herb Croutons
19 Herb Croutons
20 Cajun Chicken Caesar
21 Chili Prawn Caesar
22 Bacon and Egg Salad with Dijon Vinaigrette
24 BLT Salad with Shallot Dressing
25 Greek Pasta Salad

Sandwiches

26 BGOT Grilled Cheese
27 Balsamic Beef Panini
28 Balsamic Wine Sauce
29 Mediterranean Vegetable Panini
30 Meatball Panini

Soups

31 Ginger Chicken Noodle Soup
32 Manhattan Clam Chowder
33 Corn and Chili Chowder
34 Spicy Sausage and Red Potato Chowder

Classic Caesar Salad with Herb Croutons

This light, lemony Caesar makes a great base for Cajun Chicken (p. 20) or Chili Prawns (p. 21).

If using a head of romaine lettuce, trim 2 inches (5 cm) off the base and discard it. Wash, dry, and rip (or chop) lettuce into 2-inch (5 cm) square pieces, then cover and refrigerate. Just before serving, toss lettuce in a large bowl with dressing and ¼ cup (60 mL) Parmesan cheese; add croutons and toss again. Portion out the salads, dividing the greens among 4 plates, and top each one with 1 tablespoon (15 mL) Parmesan cheese.

Classic Caesar Dressing

Whisk lemon juice with garlic and seasonings in a small bowl; gradually whisk in oil. Cover and refrigerate for 1 to 2 hours to blend the flavours. Keeps for 2 weeks refrigerated.

7 oz (200 g) package romaine lettuce leaves, or 1 large head of romaine lettuce

1 recipe Classic Caesar Dressing (p. 18)

½ cup (125 mL) grated Parmesan cheese, divided

1 cup (250 mL) Herb Croutons (p. 19)

Serves 4.

Per serving: 447 cals, 39.6 g fat, 10 mg cholesterol, 763 mg sodium, 14.4 g carbs, 8 g protein

Beverage Suggestion: Sauvignon Blanc wine or pale ale beer

Classic Caesar Dressing

2 Tbsp (30 mL) lemon juice

¾ tsp (4 mL) minced or puréed garlic

½ tsp (2 mL) salt

¼ tsp (1 mL) pepper

1½ tsp (7 mL) Worcestershire sauce

¼ tsp (1 mL) dry mustard

½ cup (125 mL) canola oil

Makes ⅔ cup (160 mL), or enough for 4 first-course salads.

Per Tbsp (15 mL): 91 cals, 9.9 g fat, 0.7 g sat. fat, 115 mg sodium, 0.4 g carbs

Herb Croutons

This recipe is not an exact science; the measurements are estimates. Season and oil the croutons sufficiently or they won't be very tasty. If seasoned well, they make a great snack; they taste just like garlic toast!

Preheat the oven to 375°F (190°C). Place bread cubes in a medium bowl and drizzle with 2 tablespoons (30 mL) of the oil. Stir them up and drizzle with another 2 tablespoons (30 mL) of the oil before stirring again. The idea is to coat them evenly with oil so the seasoning will stick. Drizzle with remaining oil and stir once more. Sprinkle cubes evenly with half of each seasoning. Stir them up again and sprinkle them again with remaining seasoning.

Bake seasoned bread cubes on a baking sheet for 10 minutes. Remove from the oven and stir again before returning to the oven for another 5 to 8 minutes, baking until golden brown.

Cool croutons completely on a rack, then store in an airtight container for 3 to 4 days, or freeze them for up to 1 month.

2 cups (500 mL) 1-inch (2.5 cm) white bread cubes, made from a French baguette or an Italian loaf

⅓ cup (80 mL) olive oil, preferably in a bottle with a pour spout

¼ tsp (1 mL) garlic salt in a shaker

¼ tsp (1 mL) pepper in a shaker or grinder

½ tsp (2 mL) dried oregano leaves, loose or in a shaker

Makes 2 cups (500 mL).

Per ¼ cup (60 mL) (about 8 croutons): 132 cals, 9.2 g fat, 1.2 g sat. fat, 216 mg sodium, 10.8 g carbs, 1.4 g protein

Cajun Chicken Caesar

This makes a great weekend lunch (or even dinner); prepare the salad dressing and chicken ahead for easy and fast assembly.

two 8 oz (225 g) boneless and skinless chicken breasts
1½ tsp (7 mL) Creole Seasoning (p. 73)
spray oil for the grill or skillet
1 recipe Classic Caesar Salad (p. 18)

Serves 4.

Per serving: 565 cals, 41 g fat, 5.9 g sat. fat, 75 mg cholesterol, 1014 mg sodium, 14.7 g carbs, 34.3 g protein

Beverage Suggestion:
Chardonnay wine, lager beer, or citrus cocktail

Preheat the grill on medium-high. Slice chicken breasts in half horizontally to make four ½-inch (2.5 cm) thick pieces. Sprinkle all sides with Creole Seasoning to coat well. Spray the grill lightly with oil.

Place coated chicken slices on the grill; cook 3 to 4 minutes per side. Chicken should be well marked by the grill and firm to the touch when cooked through; do not overcook. Transfer chicken to a heatproof bowl, cover with a lid, and let sit for at least 10 minutes before slicing.

Prepare salad and portion onto 4 plates. Slice chicken ½ inch (2.5 cm) thick and fan out one-quarter of slices on top of each salad. Serve immediately.

Chili Prawn Caesar

A seafood lover's version and even easier than Cajun Chicken Caesar (p. 20)! Another favourite at the Decadence Café way back when.

Rinse prawns with cold water; drain well. Place prawns in a medium bowl with lime juice and chili-garlic sauce; toss gently but thoroughly to mix well. Prepare salad and portion onto 4 serving plates. Top each salad with one-quarter of the prawns, 6 or 7 per plate if using 26/30-count prawns.

1 lb (500 g) cooked, peeled, and de-veined prawns, preferably 26/30-count, tails removed

2 Tbsp (30 mL) lime juice

1 tsp (5 mL) Chinese chili-garlic sauce

1 recipe Classic Caesar Salad (p. 18)

Serves 4.

Per serving: 551 cals, 40.8 g fat, 5.8 g sat. fat, 231 mg cholesterol, 1017 mg sodium, 14.4 g carbs, 31.7 g protein

Beverage Suggestion:
Sauvignon Blanc, Mexican beer or lime Margarita

Bacon and Egg Salad with Dijon Vinaigrette

This salad may sound crazy but it is fantastic and the Dijon goes exceptionally well with the eggs! It can be quickly finished and assembled if you make the dressing ahead and pre-poach the eggs. The dressing is also a good match for a green salad with apple, pear, or chicken!

In a medium bowl, whisk together all the dressing ingredients except oil until salt and sugar are dissolved, about 1 to 2 minutes. Gradually whisk in oil until incorporated. The dressing can be made ahead to this point and covered and refrigerated for up to 3 days.

About 30 minutes before serving, take eggs out of the fridge (and dressing if prepared ahead). In a medium saucepan, cook bacon for 8 to 10 minutes on medium-high heat, stirring occasionally, until lightly browned and fat is crisp. Drain bacon well by wrapping it in a paper towel.

While bacon is cooking, bring a medium-large pot of water to a boil on medium-high heat.

Divide lettuce among 4 salad plates and sprinkle each with one-quarter cooked bacon pieces.

Gently place poached eggs in the boiling water for 1 minute to heat through. Remove immediately with a slotted spoon, drain well, and place 1 egg atop each salad. Spoon 2 tablespoons (30 mL) dressing over each egg and serve immediately.

Salad

4 large eggs, pre-poached with soft yolks and chilled

1 recipe Dijon Vinaigrette

7 oz (200 g) package romaine leaves, cleaned, dried, and torn into 2-inch (5 cm) squares

8 oz (250 g) thick-slice side bacon, about 8 slices, chopped into ½-inch (1.25 cm) pieces

Dijon Vinaigrette

2 Tbsp (30 mL) white balsamic vinegar

2 Tbsp (30 mL) minced shallot, about 1 medium

1 Tbsp (15 mL) Dijon mustard

½ tsp (2 mL) salt

½ tsp (2 mL) pepper

2 tsp (10 mL) sugar

⅓ cup (80 mL) olive oil

Serves 4.

Per serving: 575 cals, 56.1 g fat, 16 g sat. fat, 248 mg cholesterol, 714 mg sodium, 5.1 g carbs, 12.5 g protein

Beverage Suggestion: Mimosa cocktail

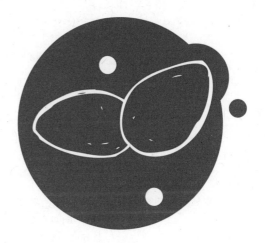

Poaching Eggs

Fresh, cold eggs poach the best.

Bring the water to a boil, then reduce the heat to keep it just below the boiling point. Next add the vinegar.

Crack each egg individually into a small measuring cup or bowl just before you add it to the water.

As you slide each egg into the hot water, use a wooden spoon to gently form the egg white into a round mass around the yolk while the white cooks. This helps keep it together and creates a nicely shaped poached egg. Work quickly when adding the eggs to the water to ensure that they all cook for about the same period of time.

When you add each egg to the water, increase the heat by a fraction to keep the water hot and almost boiling. If the water is boiling rapidly, the whites tend to turn out rubbery so it's important to keep the water at the right temperature.

If you have several eggs in the same pot, you may not be able to tell which egg is which. Cook them for 3 minutes for runny yolks and soft-cooked whites.

If the edges are ragged after cooking, eggs can be trimmed and shaped with scissors.

BLT Salad with Shallot Dressing

This Bacon Lettuce Tomato salad requires a fork and knife to tackle its great taste. I suggest Italian pancetta but you can substitute thinly sliced back bacon.

BLT Salad

4 cups (1 L) or about 4 oz (125 g) mixed greens, washed and dried

8 thin slices pancetta

2 large beefsteak tomatoes, tops and bottoms trimmed (see tip)

Shallot Dressing

2 Tbsp (30 mL) balsamic vinegar

2 Tbsp (30 mL) minced shallot, about 1 medium

½ tsp (2 mL) Dijon mustard

¼ tsp (2 mL) salt

⅛ tsp (1 mL) pepper

2 tsp (10 mL) sugar

¼ cup (60 mL) canola oil

¼ cup (60 mL) olive oil

Per serving with 3 Tbsp (45 mL) dressing: 374 cals, 34.7 g fat, 5.4 g sat. fat, 12 mg cholesterol, 400 mg sodium, 9.4 g carbs, 5.9 g protein

Beverage Suggestion: Chardonnay, Viognier or Pale Ale beer

Preheat the oven to 350°F (180°C) and line a large baking sheet with parchment paper.

Lay pancetta slices individually on the parchment so they don't overlap.

Bake for 10 minutes and then flip each slice and bake for 5 minutes more.

Slice trimmed tomatoes into 8 slices.

For the dressing, whisk together the first 6 ingredients in a medium bowl until salt and sugar are dissolved, about 1 to 2 minutes. Using the whisk, stir in oils but don't whisk dressing at this stage or it will become too thick to spoon onto the salad. Dressing can be made ahead to this point; cover and refrigerate for up to 3 days. Remove dressing from the fridge 30 minutes before serving.

Divide greens among 4 salad plates and top with pancetta slice followed by tomato slice. Repeat layering. Just before serving, spoon 3 tablespoons (45 mL) dressing over each tomato stack.

Cooking Tip: Remove the top and bottom ½ inch (2.5 cm) from the tomatoes and slice up only the middle section for this recipe. The top and bottom pieces can be diced for use in Fresh Salsa (p. 127) or another recipe.

Greek Pasta Salad

Everyone has a favourite pasta salad; our catering clients loved this one! You'll find Greek Seasoning in the spice section at the grocery store.

Fill a large stockpot with water; add salt and bring to a boil on high heat. Add pasta to boiling water; stir well. Cook pasta according to package directions, stirring occasionally to prevent pasta from sticking to the bottom of the pot.

After pasta has cooked for recommended time, test for doneness by tasting a piece. Pasta should be tender but not too chewy (dente) for the salad. If too dente, cook 1 to 2 minutes more and retest.

When desired tenderness is reached, drain pasta and rinse with cold water to stop the cooking and to rinse off salt. Place pasta in a large bowl; cool completely.

For the dressing, whisk together all ingredients except the oil in a medium bowl. Whisk well to dissolve sugar and salt. Add oil gradually; whisk to incorporate. If making the dressing ahead, cover and refrigerate for up to 2 weeks.

Toss pasta with dressing and vegetables, stirring to coat well with dressing. Cover and refrigerate until just before serving.

To serve, add ½ cup (125 mL) feta; toss well. Sprinkle remaining feta on top of salad and serve.

Cooking Tip: The salt added to the pasta water helps to keep the pasta from sticking together.

Pasta Salad

1 lb (500 g) package dried fusilli, small penne, or rotini

1 Tbsp (15 mL) salt for pasta water (see tip)

1 cup (250 mL) diced English cucumber

1 cup (250 mL) diced Roma or beefsteak tomato

⅓ cup (80 mL) diced red onion

½ cup (125 mL) canned sliced black olives, rinsed and drained well

1 cup (250 mL) feta cheese, rinsed and drained well, divided

Greek Dressing

2 Tbsp (15 mL) red wine vinegar

2 tsp (5 mL) sugar

½ tsp (1 mL) salt

¼ tsp (1 mL) pepper

1 tsp (5 mL) Greek Seasoning

½ cup (125 mL) olive oil

½ tsp (2 mL) dried oregano leaves

1 tsp (5 mL) dried parsley flakes

Makes about 13 cups (3.25 L).

Per 1 cup (250 mL): 246 cals, 12 g fat, 3 g sat. fat, 10 mg cholesterol, 268 mg sodium, 28.3 g carbs, 6.4 g protein

Beverage Suggestion:
Sauvignon Blanc or Fumé Blanc wine, light beer

BGOT Grilled Cheese

Bacon, Green Onion, and Tomato make this grilled cheese a special treat!

2 medium Roma tomatoes

8 slices thick sandwich bread, white, brown, or sourdough

16 thin slices processed cheddar cheese, preferably Kraft Velveeta or Singles

4 slices side bacon, cooked crisp, drained, and chopped coarsely

4 green onions, coarse tops trimmed and discarded, chopped fine

¼ cup (60 mL) butter, softened

Serves 4.

Per sandwich: 648 cals, 35.3 g fat, 20.1 g sat. fat, 123 mg cholesterol, 1600 mg sodium, 60.3 g carbs, 22.3 g protein

Beverage Suggestion: ale or lager beer, Chardonnay

Preheat the oven to 250°F (120°C) to keep cooked sandwiches warm.

On a cutting board, slice Roma tomatoes lengthwise halfway between the stem and pointed end. Using your index finger, scoop out seeds from inner "pockets" of tomatoes and discard. Dice tomato flesh into ½-inch (2.5 cm) cubes; drain off any liquid and blot with paper towels to dry.

Lay out 4 slices of sandwich bread and top each one with 1 cheese slice. Divide bacon bits and green onions among the 4 slices. Add one-quarter of chopped tomato, pressing toppings down gently to help them stick together. Top each slice with a second cheese slice and a second bread slice. Butter the top of each sandwich with 1½ teaspoons (7.5 mL) butter.

Preheat a large non-stick skillet on medium-high for 2 to 3 minutes. Carefully place two sandwiches, butter side down, into the pan. Butter exposed side of each sandwich with 1½ teaspoons (7.5 mL) butter and covered for 2 to 3 minutes until sandwich bottoms are golden. Carefully flip sandwiches with a large lifter and cook second side for 2 to 3 minutes to brown. Check to see if cheese is melted inside sandwiches. If not, reduce the heat and cook for 1 to 2 minutes more. Remove sandwiches from the pan; let sit for 1 to 2 minutes before cutting. Place cooked sandwiches in the oven on a tray while you cook the other two.

Balsamic Beef Panini

This is a seriously good beef sandwich and is best cooked on a panini press. Make extra sauce to freeze in case of a craving emergency!

Preheat the panini press following the manufacturer's instructions and preheat the oven to 175°F (80°C) for keeping grilled sandwiches warm. If heating sandwiches in the oven instead of grilling, preheat the oven to 375°F (190°C).

In a small saucepan, heat sauce on medium-low until steaming. Add sliced meat; stir well. Butter insides of buns, using 2 teaspoons (10 mL) per bun, and then top with grainy mustard, about ¾ teaspoon (4 mL) per bun. Add 1 slice of cheese to each bun and top with one-quarter of the beef. Add 2 slices tomato to each bun, covering with remaining cheese slices, and then top halves of buns. Press down on each bun to pack ingredients together.

Lightly brush or spray both sides of the panini press with oil. Add sandwiches to the preheated press—likely 2 will fit at a time. Cook panini until golden, about 4 to 5 minutes. Keep first 2 sandwiches warm in the oven until you have the second batch done. If you are heating sandwiches in the oven, wrap each one individually in a sealed foil packet; bake for 20 minutes or until heated through and cheese is melted.

1 recipe Balsamic Wine Sauce (p. 28)

8 oz (225 g) cooked prime rib roast beef, thinly sliced and cut into 1 × 2-inch (2.5 × 5 cm) strips

4 ciabatta, or other Italian-style buns, sliced

8 tsp (40 mL) butter, softened

2 Tbsp (30 mL) grainy Dijon mustard

8 slices Roma tomato, about
2 medium tomatoes

8 slices (about 6 oz [175 g]) Edam, Monterey Jack, or white cheddar cheese

vegetable oil or non-stick spray oil if using a panini press, or aluminum foil if wrapping sandwiches to heat in the oven

Serves 4, very well indeed.

Per sandwich: 487 cals, 27 g fat, 13.2 g sat. fat, 83 mg cholesterol, 1161 mg sodium, 29.8 g carbs, 31.1 g protein

Beverage Suggestion:
dark beer, ale, or lager, Merlot or Pinot Noir

Balsamic Wine Sauce

Try this sauce drizzled over hot roast beef or grilled steak.

2 Tbsp (30 mL) balsamic vinegar
2 cups (500 mL) low-sodium beef stock
¼ cup (60 mL) dry red wine
¼ tsp (1 mL) salt
¼ tsp (1 mL) pepper
1 tsp (5 mL) sugar

Makes ½ cup (125 mL).
Per 2 Tbsp (30 mL): 14 cals,
897 mg sodium, 3.6 g carbs

In a medium saucepan, heat vinegar, beef stock, and wine on medium-high. Bring mixture to a boil and cook until liquid is reduced to ½ cup (125 mL) in volume, about 15 minutes. Add seasonings in the last few minutes of cooking to dissolve salt and sugar. If you are making the sauce ahead, cool, cover, and refrigerate for up to 2 days, or freeze in a small airtight container for up to 2 months (but I doubt you will wait that long to use it).

Mediterranean Vegetable Panini

Robust, satisfying flavours for any time of the year!

Preheat the panini press following the manufacturer's instructions and preheat the oven to 175°F (80°C) for keeping grilled sandwiches warm. If heating sandwiches in the oven instead of grilling, preheat the oven to 375°F (190°C).

In a large non-stick skillet, heat 1 tablespoon (15 mL) olive oil on medium-high. Fry eggplant slices until soft and lightly browned on one side, about 2 to 3 minutes. Flip and brown other side for about 1 minute; transfer slices to a plate. Repeat until all slices are cooked, adding 1 tablespoon (15 mL) oil to the pan for each subsequent round of frying.

After eggplant is done, heat remaining olive oil in the same skillet on medium-high. Add mushrooms, onions, garlic, lemon juice, and seasonings; stir well. Cook mixture, stirring occasionally, until all moisture has evaporated from the mushrooms and onions are golden brown, about 10 minutes. Remove from heat.

In a small bowl, mix pesto with mayonnaise; stir well. Spread each bun with 1 tablespoon (15 mL) pesto mayo, then add 1 cheese slice. Top with one-quarter of the mushroom/onion mixture, one-quarter of the eggplant, one-quarter of the roasted red peppers, and a second cheese slice. Close buns and press down firmly to pack ingredients together.

Lightly brush or spray both sides of the panini press with oil. Add sandwiches to the preheated grill—likely 2 will fit at a time. Grill panini until golden, about 4 to 5 minutes. Keep first 2 sandwiches warm in the oven until you have the second batch done. If you are heating sandwiches in the oven, wrap each one individually in a sealed foil packet; bake for 20 minutes or until heated through and cheese is melted.

1 medium-large eggplant, peeled and sliced lengthwise, ¼ inch (6 mm) thick

¼ cup (60 mL) olive oil, or olive oil spray

1 small to medium sweet onion, quartered then sliced thin (about 2 cups [500 mL])

2 cups (500 mL) mushrooms, sliced ¼ inch (6 mm) thick

½ tsp (2 mL) minced garlic

1 tsp (5 mL) lemon juice

¼ tsp (1 mL) salt

¼ tsp (1 mL) pepper

1 cup (250 mL) roasted red peppers (2 whole or 4 halves), rinsed, drained, and dried

6 oz (175 g) mozzarella cheese, sliced thin

4 ciabatta, or other Italian-style buns, sliced

2 Tbsp (30 mL) basil pesto

⅓ cup (80 mL) whole egg mayonnaise such as Hellman's or Kraft Real Mayo

vegetable oil or non-stick spray oil if using a panini press, or aluminum foil if wrapping sandwiches to heat in the oven

Serves 4.

Per sandwich: 575 cals, 38.5 g fat, 9.1 g sat. fat, 40 mg cholesterol, 935 mg sodium, 40.5 g carbs, 16.3 g protein

Beverage Suggestion:
Chardonnay, Merlot or Pinot Noir

Meatball Panini

My version of an Italian classic; guys absolutely love this one!

½ recipe Meatballs and Marinara (p. 86)
4 ciabbata, or other Italian-style buns, sliced
6 oz (175 g) thin-sliced mozzarella cheese
vegetable oil or non-stick spray oil if using
a panini press, or aluminum foil if wrapping
sandwiches to heat in the oven

Serves 4.

Per sandwich: 392 cals, 15 g fat, 7.3 g sat. fat,
79 mg cholesterol, 1091 mg sodium,
38.4 g carbs, 25.9 g protein

Beverage Suggestion:
pale ale beer, dark lager, Chianti

Preheat the panini press following the manufacturer's instructions and preheat the oven to 175°F (80°C) for keeping grilled sandwiches warm. If heating sandwiches in the oven instead of grilling, preheat the oven to 375°F (190°C).

Remove meatballs from Marinara sauce; make sure they are well coated but not dripping with sauce. (Extra sauce can be used as a dip for the sandwiches or saved for another use.)

Add 1 cheese slice to each bun and top with one-quarter of the meatballs, about 4 or 5 per sandwich, and then a second cheese slice. Close buns and press down firmly to pack ingredients together.

Lightly brush or spray both sides of the panini press with oil. Add sandwiches to the preheated grill—likely 2 will fit at a time. Grill panini until golden, about 4 to 5 minutes. Keep first 2 sandwiches warm in the oven until you have the second batch done. If you are heating the sandwiches in the oven, wrap each sandwich individually in a sealed foil packet; bake for 20 minutes or until heated through and cheese is melted.

Ginger Chicken Noodle Soup

If you like ginger, you will love this Asian-style chicken noodle soup. It is a must if you are craving chicken noodle soup, or if you are trying to cure what ails you.

Prepare chicken as in Cajun Chicken Caesar (p. 20) but leave unseasoned. After cutting chicken into strips, crosscut several times again to make ½-inch (1 cm) cubes.

In a large stockpot, heat stock on medium-high. Add mushrooms, onions, and seasoning; cook for 8 to 10 minutes, until mushrooms are soft.

Bring mixture to a boil, add noodles, and cook for 5 minutes more. Lower the heat to medium-low and add chicken. Check soup to see if any salt is needed, which will depend on stock used; if soup tastes flat, the additional salt is needed. Portion soup into bowls; garnishing each one with 1 to 1½ teaspoons (5 to 7 mL) cilantro.

Cooking Tip: If you are not using "instant" egg noodles, cook the noodles first before adding them to the soup.

1½ lb (750 g) boneless and skinless chicken breasts, cooked (p. 20)

1 lb (500 g) mushrooms, sliced ¼ inch (6 mm) thick

8 cups (2 L) low-sodium chicken stock

1 bunch green onions, coarse top ends trimmed and discarded, chopped

2 Tbsp (30 mL) soy sauce

1 Tbsp (15 mL) minced fresh ginger

1 Tbsp (15 mL) minced garlic

½ tsp (2 mL) pepper

4 oz (125 g) instant Asian egg noodles (see Cooking Tip), blocks broken into several chunks each

¼ to ½ tsp (1 to 2 mL) salt, to taste (optional)

¼ cup (60 mL) minced cilantro leaves

Makes 12 cups (3 L).

Per 1 cup (250 mL): 100 cals, 1.1 g fat, 0.2 g sat. fat, 34 mg cholesterol, 373 mg sodium, 10.3 g carbs, 12.2 g protein

Beverage Suggestion:
Pinot Grigio—unless you're actually sick, in which case I suggest drinking lot of clear fluids and what could be better than more ginger, namely the kind found in ice cold ginger ale!

Manhattan Clam Chowder

You see cream-based clam chowder on both Canadian and American coasts. This version is low in fat and economical to make. It was a daily favourite among the neighbourhood office workers eating at our restaurant, the Decadence Café, in Victoria, BC, in the nineties.

1 ⅓ cups (330 mL) diced celery

½ cup (125 mL) diced onion

1 tsp (5 mL) minced garlic

2 Tbsp (30 mL) minced fresh parsley leaves, or substitute dried flakes

2 tsp (10 mL) salt

1 ½ tsp (7 mL) pepper

½ tsp (2 mL) ground thyme

½ tsp (2 mL) ground savory

1 Tbsp (15 mL) sugar

1 bay leaf

1 lb (500 g) potatoes, scrubbed and cut into 1-inch (2.5 cm) cubes

5.5 oz (156 mL) can tomato paste whisked together with 2 cups (500 mL) water

½ cup (125 mL) flour whisked with 1 cup (250 mL) cold water just before using

12 oz (355 mL) can baby clams, drained and rinsed

Makes 12 cups (3 L).

Per 1 cup (250 mL): 88 cals, 0.7 g fat, 0.1 g sat. fat, 17 mg cholesterol, 546 mg sodium, 14.1 g carbs, 6.5 g protein

Beverage Suggestion:
pale ale or lager beer, Sauvignon Blanc

In a large pot or stockpot, cook celery, onion, and potato in 2 cups (500 mL) water on medium-high heat. Bring the mixture to a boil, cover, and cook for 8 to 10 minutes until vegetables are tender. The heat can be reduced gradually to medium; keep the mixture hot enough to continue cooking at a low boil. Add garlic, seasoning, sugar, and watered-down tomato paste; stir well to combine.

Soup should be hot but not boiling when adding the flour mixture; if necessary, remove pot from heat and wait until it stops. Strain flour mixture through a sieve into the soup, whisking constantly to prevent lumps. Cook on medium-low heat to thicken soup and cook the flour. Soup will thicken quite quickly if the mixture is really hot. After the soup has thickened, reduce to a simmer and add clams; mix well. Soup can simmer for up to 30 minutes; stir occasionally to prevent sticking.

Corn and Chili Chowder

This chowder has wonderful chili flavour; I would call it spicy (mild) but not hot.

In a large saucepan or stockpot, on medium-high heat, cook onion in 2 cups (500 mL) water until transparent, about 8 to 10 minutes. Add corn and garlic; cook for another 5 to 10 minutes. Add whipping cream, chilies, and another 2 cups (500 mL) water. Cook mixture on medium heat until steaming but not boiling, about 5 to 7 minutes. Add the flour/water mixture through a sieve and whisk immediately. Continue cooking on medium heat, whisking frequently, until soup is thickened, about 7 to 10 minutes. Whisk in the seasoning and herbs to prevent clumping. Soup can be made ahead and reheated slowly, stirring frequently with a whisk, on medium-low.

Cooking Tip: You can substitute purchased canned or frozen corn but I suggest buying young or "baby" corn so the kernels are tender.

1/3 cup (80 mL) onion, finely diced

2½ cups (625 mL) fresh corn kernels (from 3 or 4 cobs; see Cooking Tip [p. 40])

1 tsp (5 mL) minced garlic

1 cup (250 mL) whipping cream

¼ cup (60 mL) (half 4.5 oz [127 g] can) green Mexican chilies, minced

2 tsp (10 mL) salt

½ tsp (2 mL) pepper

1 Tbsp (15 mL) finely minced fresh parsley leaves, or substitute dried flakes

1/3 cup (80 mL) flour whisked with 1 cup (250 mL) water until smooth

Makes 9 cups (2.25 L), which serves 6 with 1½-cup (375 mL) servings or 9 with 1-cup (250 mL) servings.

Per 1 cup (250 mL): 153 cals, 9.8 g fat, 5.9 g sat. fat, 35 mg cholesterol, 567 mg sodium, 13.4 g carbs, 2.6 g protein

Beverage Suggestion: White Sangria, Mexican beer

Spicy Sausage and Red Potato Chowder

There is something about this soup; it is *sooo* delicious, plus super-hearty with a kick!

½ lb (250 g) hot Italian sausages (about 3), casings removed and meat crumbled

1½ lb (750 g) red potatoes, cut into 1-inch (2.5 cm) cubes

1 tsp (5 mL) salt for the potato water

1 cup (250 mL) whipping cream

½ tsp (2 mL) minced garlic

5.5 oz (170 mL) pale ale beer (½ a bottle; the other half is for the cook!)

2 tsp (10 mL) salt

½ tsp (2 mL) pepper

2 Tbsp (30 mL) finely minced fresh parsley leaves, or substitute dried flakes

½ cup (125 mL) flour whisked with 1 cup (250 mL) cold water

1½ cups (375 mL) grated Edam or Monterey cheese

Makes 9 cups (2.25 L), which serves 6 with 1½-cup (375 mL) servings or 9 with 1-cup (250 mL) servings.

Per 1 cup (250 mL): 341 cals, 23.4 g fat, 11.6 g sat. fat, 67 mg cholesterol, 880 mg sodium, 21.6 g carbs, 10.9 g protein

Beverage Suggestion: dark lager, wheat beer, Chardonnay

In a medium non-stick skillet, cook sausage meat on medium heat, stirring occasionally, until no longer pink, about 5 to 7 minutes. Drain well on paper towels.

Fill a large saucepan with 8 cups (2 L) water. Add potatoes and salt; bring to a boil on high heat. Reduce heat to medium gradually but retain a boil. Cook potatoes until tender but still firm, about 8 to 10 minutes; don't overcook. Drain well and set aside.

In a large saucepan or stockpot, cook whipping cream, beer, and 4 cups (1 L) water on medium-high heat until steaming but not boiling, about 5 minutes. Add the flour/water mixture through a sieve to prevent lumps; whisk the mixture immediately. Continue to stir constantly as soup will thicken quickly. Reduce heat to medium-low; add cheese and stir until melted. Add sausage and potatoes; mix well.

Small Bites

36 Blackened Scallops
   with Honey Lime Butter

37 Bruschetta

38 Chili Cheese Croquettes

39 Crab Stuffed Mushroom Caps

40 Corn and Cheddar Fritters

41 Damn Good Prawns

42 Mardi Gras Grilled Prawns

43 Mushroom Crostini

44 Hot Italian Sausage Rolls
   with Honey Lemon Dijon Dip

45 Honey Lemon Dijon Dip

46 Coconut Prawns with Mango Sauce

47 Mango Sauce

48 The Ultimate Popcorn Shrimp

49 Mexican Beef Dip with Chips

50 Grilled Chicken Quesadillas

51 Mussels with Lime Cilantro Sauce

52 Taquitos with Guacamole Sauce

53 Guacamole Sauce

Blackened Scallops with Honey Lime Butter

Spicy and sweet with a little heat! Purchase 1¼ lb (625 g) fresh scallops, or use 15/20-count frozen ones.

3 Tbsp (45 mL) lime juice
¼ cup (60 mL) dry white wine
3 Tbsp (45 mL) honey
18 medium-large scallops, at room temperature
2 Tbsp (30 mL) Creole Seasoning (p. 73), in a small bowl
¾ cup (185 mL) butter, divided

Serves 6.
Per 3 scallops and 2 Tbsp (30 mL) sauce:
345 cals, 24.7 g fat, 204 mg cholesterol,
615 mg sodium, 10.8 g carbs, 19.6 g protein

Beverage Suggestion:
Sauvignon Blanc white wine

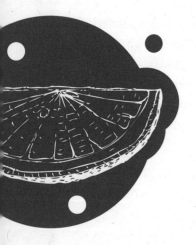

In a medium skillet, bring lime juice and wine to a boil on medium-high heat; cook until only about 2 tablespoons (30 mL) of liquid is left, about 5 minutes. Add honey; mix until smooth. You can make the sauce to this point, cover, and refrigerate until 20 minutes before serving.

Dip tops and bottoms of scallops in Creole Seasoning, coating the surface of each one. Heat a large non-stick skillet on high until very hot, about 2 to 3 minutes. Add 2 tablespoons (30 mL) butter; immediately add scallops, searing them for 1 to 2 minutes, or until very dark brown. Add another 2 tablespoons (30 mL) butter to the skillet. Turn scallops quickly; sear the second side for 1 minute. Remove seared scallops from heat, cover, and let stand 5 minutes to cook their centres.

Start warming lime sauce in a medium skillet on low, then gradually whisk in ½ cup (125 mL) butter. Spoon 2 tablespoons (30 mL) honey lime butter onto 6 plates and top with 3 scallops.

Bruschetta

A classic Italian starter; healthy and economical. I haven't met anyone who doesn't like it. Make larger ones and serve them with soup or salad for a delicious lunch.

In a medium bowl, mix together the first 6 ingredients with 1 tablespoon (15 mL) olive oil. Cover and refrigerate topping for 2 to 3 hours.

Just before serving, preheat the broiler to 500°F (260°C) and brush top side of bread slices lightly with 3 tablespoons (45 mL) olive oil. Place on an ungreased baking sheet in the top third of the oven (but not directly under the broiler) and broil for 1 to 2 minutes to lightly brown them.

Place Bruschetta topping in a medium-large non-stick skillet and heat on medium-low for 3 to 4 minutes, stirring occasionally to warm through. Do not overcook—mixture should remain raw and crunchy. Evenly spread each piece of baguette with 1 tablespoon (15 mL) topping and sprinkle with ½ teaspoon (2 mL) Parmesan cheese. Serve immediately while still warm to bring out the flavours.

1½ cups (375 mL) diced tomatoes, preferably Romas

¾ cup (185 mL) onion, minced

1 tsp (5 mL) minced garlic

¼ cup (60 mL) fresh basil leaves, finely chopped (or substitute 1 Tbsp [15 mL] basil pesto or purée)

¼ tsp (1 mL) salt

¼ tsp (1 mL) pepper

¼ cup (60 mL) olive oil, divided

French baguette, sliced crosswise ½ inch (1 cm) thick to yield 36 slices

⅓ cup (80 mL) finely grated Parmesan cheese

Makes 36 appetizers.

Per appetizer: 47 cals, 1.9 g fat, 0.4 g sat. fat, 1 mg cholesterol, 105 mg sodium, 6 g carbs, 1.2 g protein

Beverage Suggestion:
light, dry red wine, such as Merlot, Pinot Noir, or Beaujolais

Chili Cheese Croquettes

These appies will disappear like magic and everyone will immediately be asking for more!!! Start making them early because there is some freezer time required prior to your breading them.

1 lb (500 g) Edam or Monterey Jack cheese, grated

4.5 oz (127 g) can diced mild green chilies, rinsed, drained, and dried with paper towels

½ tsp (2 mL) pepper

waxed paper for wrapping cheese logs

½ to ¾ cup (125 mL to 185 mL) flour

2 large eggs, at room temperature

2 cups (500 mL) Panko breadcrumbs

1 to 1½ cups (250 to 375 mL) vegetable oil for deep-frying

1 recipe Fresh Salsa (p. 127) or substitute purchased deli-style salsa (optional)

Makes 40 croquettes.

Per croquette (without salsa): 86 cals, 5.2 g fat, 2 g sat. fat, 19 mg cholesterol, 148 mg sodium, 5.8 g carbs, 3.8 g protein

Beverage Suggestion: lime margarita; Corona or Dos Equis beer

In a medium-large bowl, mix together cheese, chilies, and pepper. Tightly pack and press five ½-cup (125 mL) portions of cheese mixture into logs measuring 1 inch (2.5 cm) wide and 7 inches (18 cm) long. Roll logs in waxed paper, place in a covered container, and freeze until firm, about 1 to 2 hours.

Remove logs from freezer when you are ready to bread them (up to 1 day ahead). Cut each log into 5 equal pieces to make 40 pieces total. Place flour in one medium bowl, eggs (beaten) in another, and breadcrumbs in a third. Dip each cheese piece in flour to thoroughly coat it, and then set aside on a plate. When all pieces are coated with flour, dip several pieces at a time into beaten egg; turn to coat well. Using a strainer spoon, lift out 1 to 2 pieces cheese; drain off excess egg, then add to bowl with breadcrumbs. With a soupspoon, scoop crumbs over cheese pieces to coat them thoroughly. Repeat process until all pieces are breaded. Refrigerate breaded cheese pieces, uncovered, for at least 30 minutes before frying. At this point, croquettes can be layered between wax paper and frozen in a covered container for up to 1 month.

In a large non-stick skillet, preheat oil on medium-high to 375°F (190°C), or until rippling but not smoking. Fry croquettes for 1 to 2 minutes until golden; flip with a heatproof spoon and brown other side for 1 to 2 minutes. Drain croquettes briefly on paper towels, then transfer to a platter until they are all cooked. Serve with salsa on the side, if desired.

Crab Stuffed Mushroom Caps

This recipe was on every catering menu at Decadence Catering over the years because people asked for them regularly. Never any leftovers with this one!

Place mushroom caps underside down on a paper-towel-lined dinner plate. Microwave mushrooms on medium-high for 2 minutes. Feel the mushrooms to see if they have softened and look to see if they have released any water. If not, microwave for 1-minute intervals until mushrooms are soft and pliable, caps have shrunk in size, and paper towel is fairly wet with mushroom juice. (This step is included because mushrooms have very high water content. If you don't precook them, they will be watery when served—especially the filling. We have all experienced the mushroom juice that runs down your arm when you bite into a cap!) Cool mushroom caps underside down to drain off any liquid, then pat insides with paper towels to dry.

Place cream cheese, Worcestershire sauce, lemon juice, and seasonings in a medium bowl; mix well with a wooden spoon until completely combined and smooth. Add crabmeat and stir to combine. Fill each mushroom cap with 1 tablespoon (15 mL) filling, using more or less depending on size of mushroom. Top each filled cap with 1 teaspoon (5 mL) grated cheese.

Preheat the oven to 375°F (190°C) and position a rack in the middle of the oven. Space mushroom caps about 1 inch (2.5 cm) apart on a baking sheet that is lightly oiled or lined with parchment. Bake mushroom caps for 10 to 15 minutes to heat through, until lightly browned on top and filling is bubbling. Cool for 5 minutes before serving.

24 medium-large mushrooms
(about 1½ lb [750 g]), stems removed

4 oz (125 g) regular cream cheese,
at room temperature

¾ tsp (4 mL) Worcestershire sauce

½ tsp (2 mL) lemon juice

¼ tsp (1 mL) dry mustard

¼ tsp (1 mL) salt

¼ tsp (1 mL) pepper

⅛ tsp (0.5 mL) cayenne pepper

4 oz (120 g) can crabmeat, drained well

½ cup (125 mL) grated Edam
or Monterey Jack cheese

vegetable oil, non-stick spray oil,
or parchment paper for baking sheet

Makes 24.

Per 3 mushroom caps: 105 cals, 7.6 g fat,
4.2 g sat. fat, 34 mg cholesterol,
231 mg sodium, 2.5 g carbs, 6.7 g protein

Beverage Suggestion:
fruity, dry white wine, such as
Riesling or Gewürztraminer

Corn and Cheddar Fritters

Addictive little things that are a wonderful way to use up leftover cooked fresh corn. A great starter with Southern food, such as Debbie Fried Chicken (p. 74).

2 cups (500 mL) cooked sweet corn kernels (from 3 cobs; see Cooking Tip)

2 eggs, beaten

2 tsp (10 mL) milk or cream

1½ Tbsp (22.5 mL) melted butter

1 cup (250 mL) grated sharp or aged cheddar cheese

⅓ cup (80 mL) flour

1½ tsp (7.5 mL) sugar

¾ tsp (4 mL) salt

½ tsp (2 mL) baking powder

½ cup (125 mL) canola or corn oil

Fresh Salsa (p. 127) or purchased deli-style salsa

sour cream (optional)

Makes 45 appetizers.

Per 3 fritters (without condiments): 103 cals, 6.8 g fat, 3 g sat. fat, 40 mg cholesterol, 184 mg sodium, 6.7 g carbs, 4 g protein

Beverage Suggestion: crisp, dry white wine, such as Sauvignon Blanc or Viognier

Preheat the oven to 175°F (80°C) and line a baking sheet with paper towels.

In a large bowl, mix corn kernels with eggs, milk, butter, and cheese. In a medium bowl, sift together the dry ingredients. Stir the dry ingredients into the wet ingredients until just combined.

In a large non-stick skillet, preheat oil on medium-high for 3 to 4 minutes, or until rippling but not smoking. With a spoon, drop 1 tablespoon (15 mL) portions of batter into the oil; flatten the tops with the spoon to make 1½-inch (4 cm) rounds. Cook fritters for 1 to 2 minutes, or until golden; turn and brown the other side for 1 to 2 minutes more. Transfer fritters to baking sheet to drain and keep warm in the oven while you fry remaining fritters. Repeat process until all batter is used up.

Serve fritters warm with salsa and sour cream, if desired.

Removing kernels from fresh corn: Hold cob upright with narrow end at top and wide end placed on a cutting board. Grasping cob securely, use a sharp knife to slice off corn kernels with downward strokes. Rotate cob as you go to remove all the corn. Place kernels in a bowl and work through them with your hands to separate any ones still sticking together in rows. Remove any corn silk or husk strands and discard. You can portion corn into freezer bags or covered containers and freeze for up to 3 months. Thaw to use in recipes such as Corn and Chili Chowder (p. 33), or fry corn in a bit of butter for a side vegetable.

Damn Good Prawns

When I was trying to come up with a name for these prawns, my husband, Doug, said, "I don't know what to call them, but they are damn good." Hence their crazy name! Use 16/20-count or 21/25-count prawns for this recipe. (See Mardi Gras Prawns [p. 42] for advice on sizing and purchasing prawns.)

In a small saucepan, melt butter on medium-low heat, then add all the other ingredients except prawns and baguette. Cook for 1 to 2 minutes to dissolve salt and blend the flavours. Remove from heat. The sauce can be made ahead to this point; cool, cover, and refrigerate for up to 3 days.

Thirty minutes before cooking prawns, remove sauce from fridge and place in a small saucepan. Cook sauce on medium-low heat for 1 to 2 minutes to re-melt the butter; stir to mix and then remove from heat.

Preheat the broiler to 500°F (260°C) and place prawns and sauce in a large, shallow baking pan. Stir prawns to coat well with sauce and spread them out so they are in one layer. Broil prawns for 3 to 4 minutes. With a pair of tongs, turn them over as they turn orange and start curling somewhat. (If corner ones are cooking more quickly, move them away from the edge.) After flipping them, cook prawns for another 2 to 3 minutes until they are all orange and curled slightly; do not overcook. Remove prawns from the broiler, cover with a baking sheet or foil, and let rest for 5 minutes to finish cooking.

Serve prawns with sauce and sliced bread on the side for dipping.

⅓ cup (80 mL) butter

3 Tbsp (45 mL) olive oil

2 tsp (10 mL) chili powder

2 tsp (10 mL) coarse ground pepper

¾ tsp (4 mL) salt

1 tsp (5 mL) minced or crushed garlic (1 medium clove)

1 Tbsp plus 1 tsp (20 mL) Worcestershire sauce

1 Tbsp (15 mL) lemon juice

2 lb (1 kg) raw, deveined, easy-peel prawns, at room temperature

1 French baguette, sliced ½ inch (1 cm) thick for serving

Makes 32 to 40 pieces depending on the prawn count.

Per 4 or 5 prawns and 2 slices baguette: 288 cals, 15.1 g fat, 5.9 g sat. fat, 191 mg cholesterol, 568 mg sodium, 13.2 g carbs, 24.7 g protein

Beverage Suggestion: pale ale or lager beer

Mardi Gras Grilled Prawns

These tasty treats can also be a main course if served over pasta or rice. Use 16/20-count or 21/25-count prawns. (See Cooking Tip below for advice on sizing and purchasing prawns.)

1 lb (500 g) raw prawns, peeled and deveined, tail left on

¼ cup (60 mL) olive oil

2 Tbsp (30 mL) Creole Seasoning (p. 73)

2 Tbsp (30 mL) lemon juice

1 Tbsp (15 mL) honey

1 Tbsp (15 mL) soy sauce

French baguette, sliced ½ inch (1 cm) thick for serving

Serves 4, with 4 or 5 prawns per person.

Per 4 or 5 prawns and 2 slices baguette: 306 cals, 15 g fat, 2.1 g sat. fat, 221 mg cholesterol, 1237 mg sodium, 17.1 g carbs, 25.5 g protein

Beverage Suggestion: medium-dark beer, such as Rickard's Red

In a medium baking dish, combine all the ingredients except baguette slices; mix well. Cover and marinate for at least 1 hour in the fridge. Remove from fridge 30 minutes before cooking prawns.

Preheat the oven to 450°F (240°C). Bake prawns for 2 to 3 minutes until shells turn orange and they begin to curl. With a pair of tongs, turn them over and cook for 1 to 2 minutes more. Remove prawns from the oven, and cover with a baking sheet or aluminum foil for 5 minutes while they cook through. Transfer prawns to a platter and serve with baguette slices on the side for dipping in the spicy sauce.

Purchasing and cooking prawns: If you purchase peeled prawns instead of easy-peel ones, the cooking time will be slightly less. The shells keep the prawns moist while cooking but are fussy to deal with. If you are using the dish as a main course, I suggest peeled prawns (tail on is fine) to make the experience less messy for friends and family. For an appetizer, it may be less of a concern if finger bowls are available.

Prawns (and scallops) are sold by the number that makes up a pound; the smaller the number per pound, the larger the prawns. The label 16/20 means 16 to 20 prawns in a pound; a single 16-count prawn weighs 1 oz (30 g) and is a substantial size. If you substitute smaller prawns (e.g. 21/25 per pound), reduce the cooking time and watch them closely to prevent overcooking.

Mushroom Crostini

If you are a mushroom lover, these crostini will become your NBFF (New Best Favourite Food). One of my catering clients, M.P., begged me for this recipe a few years ago and I finally agreed—but the deal was that she would only make them when she went down south. I guess M.P. is finally free to make them anywhere now that the recipe has been published!

Slice baguette ⅓ inch (8 mm) thick on a 45° angle to yield 20 slices; set aside.

Heat oil in a large non-stick skillet on medium-high for 2 to 3 minutes; add mushrooms and stir to coat with oil. Cover and cook mushrooms for 5 minutes to sweat them so they release their moisture. Remove the lid and add lemon juice and garlic. Cook uncovered for about 5 minutes more, stirring occasionally until pan is almost dry. Add whipping cream, salt, and pepper. Bring to a boil and cook mixture for 8 to 10 minutes, stirring frequently, until cream has reduced in volume and mixture starts to thicken. (The sauce on the mushrooms should have a creamy, thick consistency.) Cool mixture to room temperature, stirring occasionally as it cools. Mushroom topping can be made ahead to this point. Cover and refrigerate for up to 3 days before use—bring to room temperature before assembling crostini.

Preheat the broiler to 500°F (260°C) and ready a baking sheet. Cut cheese into 20 wedges. Evenly spread each baguette slice with 2 teaspoons (10 mL) mushroom topping followed by a wedge of cheese. Place crostini, on the baking sheet 1 inch (2.5 cm) apart and broil on the second rack from the top of the oven for 3 to 5 minutes, or until cheese is melted and baguette edges are browned. Serve warm.

French baguette

1 Tbsp (15 mL) vegetable oil

1½ lb (750 g) mushrooms, sliced ¼ inch (6 mm) thick

1½ Tbsp (22.5 mL) lemon juice

1 tsp (5 mL) minced or puréed garlic

1½ cups (375 mL) whipping cream

1 tsp (5 mL) salt

1 tsp (5 mL) pepper

½ tsp (2 mL) ground nutmeg, preferably freshly ground

4 oz (125 g) Brie or Camembert cheese

Makes 20 crostini.

Per crostini: 115 cals, 8.1 g fat, 4.9 g sat. fat, 29 mg cholesterol, 232 mg sodium, 7.7 g carbs, 2.9 g protein

Beverage Suggestion:
Chardonnay or Viognier white wine

Hot Italian Sausage Rolls with Honey Lemon Dijon Dip

A spicy version of the old classic so a little surprising to some people!

1 lb (500 g) pork sausage meat, or plain pork sausages with casings removed

1 tsp (5 mL) Chinese chili-garlic sauce

2 tsp (4 mL) dried parsley flakes

1 tsp (5 mL) dried oregano

½ tsp (2 mL) caraway seeds

¼ tsp (1 mL) cayenne pepper

¼ tsp (1 mL) pepper

¼ tsp (1 mL) garlic salt

parchment paper for baking sheets

13 oz (400 g) package frozen puff pastry, thawed

2 to 3 Tbsp (30 to 45 mL) flour

1 large egg, beaten in a small bowl

1 recipe Honey Lemon Dijon Dip (p. 45)

Makes 48 pieces.
Per piece with 1¼ tsp (6 mL) dip: 116 cals, 11 g fat, 1.8 g sat. fat, 12 mg cholesterol, 235 mg sodium, 1.9 g carbs, 2.1 g protein

Beverage Suggestion:
pale ale or lager beer

Cooking Tip: If you have limited time, substitute good-quality hot Italian sausages (casings removed) for the meat mixture.

Using a fork or spoon, mix meat thoroughly with chili-garlic sauce, herbs, and seasonings in a medium-large bowl. Divide sausage meat into 4 equal portions and set aside.

Preheat the oven to 425°F (220°C) and line two large baking sheets with parchment. Cut pastry into 2 equal portions and dust a clean surface lightly with flour for rolling out the pastry. Using a rolling pin, press pastry into two 8- × 12-inch (20 × 30 cm) rectangles, with the long edges parallel to the edge of the counter. Slice each rectangle in half lengthwise, to make 4 narrow strips of pastry in total.

Shape sausage portions into four 12-inch (30 cm) logs and add one to each pastry strip, lining them up along the long edge closest to you. One at a time, roll each piece of pastry around its meat filling until 1 inch (2.5 cm) from far edge. Brush the exposed pastry with egg, finish rolling, and set the roll aside, seam side down. You should have a sausage roll about 1½ inches (4 cm) in diameter and 12 inches (30 cm) long. Repeat process until you have prepared all 4 rolls.

Brush a thin layer of egg over the top and sides of each roll, and then cut into 12 inch-wide (2.5 cm) slices. Place slices seam side down 2 inches (5 cm) apart on baking sheets, 24 per tray.

Bake rolls for 8 minutes, then switch and turn the trays to ensure even browning. Bake 8 minutes more, until rolls are puffed and golden, and sausage filling is firm to the touch. If rolls are slightly oily after baking, blot with paper towels. Serve warm with dip on the side.

Honey Lemon Dijon Dip

A versatile dip for breaded snacks and Hot Italian Sausage Rolls (p. 44).

In a small bowl, whisk lemon juice with honey and mustard. Stir in mayonnaise until well combined. Cover and refrigerate until 30 minutes before serving.

1 Tbsp (15 mL) lemon juice

2 Tbsp (30 mL) honey

1 Tbsp plus 1 tsp (20 mL) Dijon mustard

1 cup (250 mL) whole-egg mayonnaise such as Hellman's or Kraft Real Mayo

Makes 1¼ cups (310 mL).

Per 1 Tbsp (15 mL): 81 cals, 8.1 g fat, 0.8 g sat. fat, 4 mg cholesterol, 99 mg sodium, 1.8 g carbs, 0.2 g protein

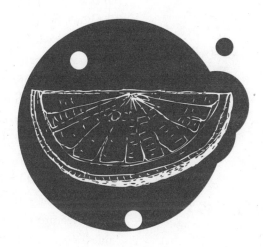

Coconut Prawns
with Mango Sauce

Holiday nostalgia results in Tropical cravings—these are for you, Greg! Use 20/24-count prawns for this recipe; thaw first if using frozen ones.

2 lb (1 kg) raw prawns, peeled and deveined, tails left on

½ tsp (2 mL) salt in a shaker or grinder

½ tsp (2 mL) pepper in a shaker or grinder

1 to 2 cups (250 to 500 mL) unsweetened medium shredded coconut

2 eggs

½ cup (125 mL) flour, in a medium bowl

1 cup (250 mL) canola oil for deep-frying

1 recipe Mango Sauce (p. 47)

Makes 40 to 48 prawns.

Per prawn (24/lb size) with 1 tsp (5 mL) dip: 46 cals, 1.7 g fat, 0.7 g sat. fat, 37 mg cholesterol, 57 mg sodium, 3.4 g carbs, 4.3 g protein

Beverage Suggestion: crisp, dry white wine, such as Fumé Blanc

Rinse prawns with cold water, drain, and then dry with paper towels. Place in a medium-large bowl and sprinkle repeatedly with salt and pepper, stirring well between additions to season them evenly.

Place 1 cup (250 mL) coconut in a medium bowl and lightly beat 1 egg in a second medium bowl (if needed later, you can add the second egg and/or top up the coconut). Line up these bowls next to the flour bowl on the counter.

Place a few prawns in the flour bowl. Stir to coat; you want the prawns to be coated with flour and dry. Shake off any excess flour and then dip each prawn in the egg, draining any excess back into the bowl. Next place the prawn in the coconut bowl and use a spoon to coat it completely with coconut, shaking off any excess back into the bowl. Set coated prawns aside on a plate. Repeat until all prawns are coated with coconut, replenishing the egg and coconut bowls partway through if necessary. Chill prawns, uncovered, for at least 30 minutes before frying so the coating adheres well.

Preheat the oil in a large non-stick deep skillet on medium-high until rippling but not smoking. Have a baking sheet ready, lined with paper towels, for draining the prawns after cooking. Test the oil temperature by dropping in a few breadcrumbs; if oil is ready, they should bubble up and brown in 30 to 60 seconds. Fry prawns in hot oil for 1 to 2 minutes, until golden and crisp on first side. With heatproof tongs, turn them as they brown and cook second side for 1 to 2 minutes more. Drain prawns on baking sheet.

Prawns are best served immediately for maximum crispness but can be kept warm in a 200 °F (95°C) oven for 5 to 10 minutes (though they may be slightly softer as a result). Serve with dip on the side.

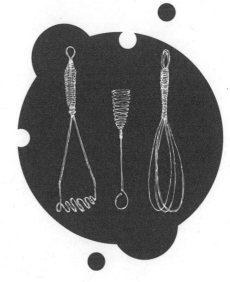

Mango Sauce

Sweet and tangy—the perfect dipping sauce for crispy bites! You will need a small food processor or a blender to purée the mangoes. To yield the 1½ cups (375 mL) mango purée needed, purchase 1½ lb (750 g) of soft, ripe fruit.

In a medium bowl, whisk together lime juice, brandy, honey, and Tabasco sauce. Add mango purée and cilantro; whisk to combine. Cover and refrigerate until needed, up to 3 days.

Cooking Tip: To ripen mangoes, place them in a paper bag with a ripe apple, at room temperature, for several days. Check them each day to determine if they are ripe enough; they should be medium-soft for slicing and very soft for puréeing (similar to avocados). Once they are ripe, you can refrigerate mangoes for 1 to 2 days longer if needed. For making mango purée, use overripe mangoes that are far too soft for slicing. The mango pulp can also be frozen in an airtight container for up to 2 months. Alternately, canned mango slices can be drained, rinsed well, and puréed to make the sauce, however, they are usually sweetened with 50% sugar syrup so it may taste sweeter.

1½ tsp (7.5 mL) lime juice

1 Tbsp (15 mL) brandy or orange-flavoured brandy

3 Tbsp (45 mL) honey

¾ tsp (7.5 mL) Tabasco sauce

3 large ripe, soft mangoes, peeled, pitted, and puréed (see Cooking Tip)

2 Tbsp (30 mL) cilantro leaves, finely minced

Makes 1¾ cups (435 mL).

Per 1½ tsp (7.5 mL): 8 cals, 1.9 g carbs

The Ultimate Popcorn Shrimp

Always a hit and very addictive!

½ lb (250 g) cooked shrimp, rinsed and dried on paper towels

1 Tbsp (15 mL) Creole Seasoning (p. 73)

½ cup (125 mL) flour, in a medium bowl

1 cup (250 mL) canola or corn oil for frying

1 recipe Cucumber Cilantro Dip (p. 57) or purchased Ranch dip (optional)

Serves 4.

2 oz (60 g) shrimp (without dip): 146 cals, 4.7 g fat, 0.4 g sat. fat, 85 mg cholesterol, 438 mg sodium, 13 g carbs, 13.2 g protein

Beverage Suggestion: light beer, such as Corona or Dos Equis

In a medium bowl, sprinkle shrimp with Creole Seasoning and toss them gently to coat thoroughly. Dredge them with flour, shaking off any excess. Let stand for 10 minutes and then dredge them again.

Heat oil in a large non-stick skillet on medium-high. Make sure oil is thoroughly hot and rippling but not smoking. Test temperature if necessary by adding one shrimp to the pan—it should bubble up immediately. Fry shrimp briefly, about 1 to 2 minutes, to turn the coating golden brown. Don't overcook—remember shrimp are already cooked.

Drain on paper towels, plate them, and serve immediately, with dip on the side if using.

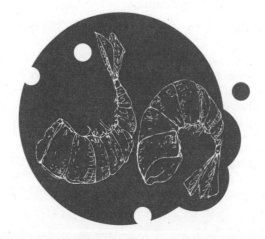

Mexican Beef Dip with Chips

A very easy, hearty meat lovers dip for casual get-togethers!

Core, seed, and mince jalapeno pepper to yield 1 tablespoon (15 mL) minced. In a large non-stick skillet, crumble beef with onion and cook on medium-high heat until meat is no longer pink and starts to brown lightly, about 8 to 10 minutes.

Add jalapeno, Worcestershire sauce, seasonings, and sugar; mix well. Stir in the sauces and lower heat to low. Cover and simmer for 45 minutes, stirring occasionally.

Just before serving, add cheese and stir until it melts. Serve with tortilla chips for scooping up the dip.

½ large jalapeno pepper

1 lb (500 g) extra-lean ground beef or veal

¼ cup (60 mL) onion, diced

¾ tsp (4 mL) Worcestershire sauce

¾ tsp (4 mL) salt

¼ tsp (1 mL) pepper

¼ tsp (1 mL) cayenne pepper

1 tsp (5 mL) sugar

¾ cup plus 2 Tbsp (215 mL) mild enchilada sauce

¼ cup plus 2 Tbsp (90 mL) tomato sauce

1 cup (250 mL) grated sharp or aged cheddar cheese

9 oz (280 g) bag salted tortilla chips

Makes 3 cups (750 mL).

Per ⅓ cup (80 mL) beef dip (without chips):
134 cals, 9.2 g fat, 3.6 g sat. fat,
37 mg cholesterol, 456 mg sodium,
2.8 g carbs, 9.9 g protein

Beverage Suggestion:
pale ale or lager beer

Grilled Chicken Quesadillas

An excellent party appetizer, or serve 3 to 4 wedges per person with a side salad for a tasty lunch. Tastes best when chicken is grilled. Purchase 1¼ lb (625 g) cheese for this recipe.

vegetable or non-stick spray oil for skillet, if using

9 cups (2.25 L) grated Edam or Monterey Jack cheese

¼ cup (60 mL) basil pesto

1¼ lb (560 g) boneless and skinless chicken breasts, cooked

⅓ cup (80 mL) minced red onion (½ medium onion)

eight 8- or 9-inch (20 or 23 cm) flour tortillas, preferably Olafson's brand

Fresh Salsa (p. 127), or substitute purchased deli-style salsa

Guacamole Sauce (p. 53), or substitute purchased guacamole

Makes 32 wedges.

Per wedge (without condiments): 181 cals, 11.9 g fat, 5.6 g sat. fat, 34 mg cholesterol, 360 mg sodium, 5.2 g carbs, 13.1 g protein

Beverage Suggestion: White sangria or margarita

Cooking Tip: To prevent tortillas from drying and curling, keep them sealed in a plastic bag while preparing quesadillas.

Preheat the grill on high, or lightly oil a 10- or 11-inch (25 or 28 cm) non-stick skillet.

In a medium-large bowl, combine cheese and pesto. Dice chicken into ½-inch (1 cm) cubes and mix with onion in a medium bowl.

Lay out 2 tortillas and top each one evenly with 1½ cups (375 mL) cheese, followed by one-quarter of the onion/chicken mixture. Top this layer with ¾ cup (185 mL) additional cheese, evenly distributed. (Second layer of cheese acts as glue when melted and holds quesadillas together during cooking.) Place a tortilla on top of each base. Stack prepared quesadillas on a dinner plate (one on top of the other) and cover with plastic wrap to prevent them from drying out. Repeat process. If using a skillet, preheat it on medium-high for 2 to 3 minutes.

Carefully place a quesadilla on the grill (2 if there is room) or in the skillet. Cook until base is golden, about 2 to 3 minutes. If grilling, check bottom for browning and good grill marks after about 2 minutes. Rotate on the grill or in the pan for even browning.

To flip and cook the other side, transfer quesadilla to a dinner plate, place another plate overtop, and turn over while holding the plates firmly together. Return quesadilla to the grill or skillet for 1 to 2 minutes to brown second side. Once cheese is fully melted inside, remove quesadilla from the grill or skillet and let stand for 5 minutes. Cut into 8 wedges and serve with salsa and guacamole on the side.

Mussels with Lime Cilantro Sauce

These mussels are a disappearing act with my seafood-loving friends and their plates are wiped clean with bread slices to get every bit of sauce. You can substitute clams for the mussels but since there will be fewer per pound, buy 2½ lb (1.25 kg). If you don't have a steamer, a large, deep, stainless steel skillet will do—just don't use any water and keep it covered while cooking.

In a small saucepan, heat lime juice and wine on medium; cook for about 1 minute, or until liquid has almost entirely evaporated. Add whipping cream, garlic, and seasoning; whisk until smooth. Add green onions and cilantro; keep sauce warm on low heat.

Check over mussels thoroughly; discard any broken ones. If any are open slightly, prod them gently with a knife to see if they close and discard if they don't. Preheat the oven to 110°F (43°C) and begin warming an ovenproof serving dish.

Fill a large steamer with 4 inches (10 cm) water and preheat on medium-high. Add mussels, cover, and cook for 2 to 3 minutes. At this point, stir mussels and then replace lid, but start checking their progress periodically. Total cooking time should be about 7 minutes, but if they were cold when you started, they may take a few minutes longer. As soon as they open, transfer mussels to the serving dish in the oven. (Removing mussels right away prevents overcooking, which can toughen them.) Discard any mussels that remain closed after 10 minutes. Toss cooked mussels with warm Lime Cilantro Sauce and serve immediately with seafood forks and baguette slices on the side for dipping.

2 lb (1 kg) fresh mussels, soaked in cold water for 30 minutes, then scrubbed and beards removed

French baguette, sliced, for serving

Lime Cilantro Sauce

2 Tbsp (30 mL) lime juice

2 Tbsp (30 mL) dry white wine

½ cup (125 mL) whipping cream

2 tsp (10 mL) minced or puréed garlic

½ tsp (2 mL) salt

¼ tsp (1 mL) pepper

½ cup (125 mL) green onion, trimmed and sliced thin (½ bunch)

2 Tbsp (30 mL) minced fresh cilantro leaves

Serves 4 as an appetizer.

Per serving (without baguette): 483 cals, 21.2 g fat, 9.2 g sat. fat, 167 mg cholesterol, 1144 mg sodium, 19.1 g carbs, 54.2 g protein

Beverage Suggestion:
smooth, dry white wine, such as Chardonnay

Taquitos with Guacamole Sauce

A more substantial version than the pencil-thin traditional ones! You'll need to make a double recipe of Guacamole Sauce (p. 53) so stock up on avocados.

1 lb (500 g) ground veal or pork

½ cup (125 mL) green onions, trimmed and finely chopped (½ bunch)

2 Tbsp (30 mL) enchilada sauce or thick salsa

½ tsp (2 mL) salt

½ tsp (2 mL) pepper

½ tsp (2 mL) minced garlic

nine 8-inch (20 cm) square spring roll wrappers

1 cup (250 mL) canola oil for deep-frying

2 cups (500 mL) Guacamole Sauce (p. 53)

Makes 27 pieces.

Per piece with 1 Tbsp (15 mL) sauce: 87 cals, 5.9 g fat, 1.4 g sat. fat, 13 mg cholesterol, 133 mg sodium, 4.4 g carbs, 3.6 g protein

Beverage Suggestion: Corona or Dos Equis beer

In a medium bowl, mix veal with green onions, enchilada sauce or salsa, seasonings, and garlic; stir well several times to combine mixture. Divide filling into 9 equal portions.

Lay a spring roll wrapper out on a cutting board and form a portion of meat into a log shape along the edge closest to you. Roll up the taquito away from you as tightly as possible. Set aside, seam side down, on a plate or the edge of the cutting board (if there is room). Repeat until all 9 rolls are assembled. Cut each roll into thirds; each piece will be about 2½ inches (6 cm) long. Clean kitchen scissors work well for this job; you may need to reshape ends of rolls after cutting.

Line a baking sheet with paper towels to drain rolls after frying. Preheat the oil in a large, deep skillet on medium-high, until rippling but not smoking. Fry rolls, seam side down, for 2 to 3 minutes, or until golden brown on the bottom. With a pair of heatproof tongs, turn taquitos over to brown the other side for 1 to 2 minutes. Check middle of rolls for doneness—meat should be brown in colour and no longer pink. Drain on a paper-towel-lined tray. Serve warm with Guacamole Sauce on the side.

Guacamole Sauce

Nature's most nutritious food, the avocado, makes the best healthy, creamy, low-calorie dip! This recipe is easily doubled or tripled.

Purée avocado with lime juice in a food processor until smooth. Add remaining ingredients and mix well to fully incorporate. If not using right away, store sauce in a plastic or glass container with a lid. To prevent browning, make sure to lay a piece of plastic wrap against the surface, and press it down along the edges of the container. Cover and refrigerate for up to 3 days.

Cooking Tip: Substitute ¼ cup (60 mL) finely chopped red onion for the green onions.

1 large avocado, peeled and pitted

1 Tbsp (15 mL) lime juice

¼ tsp (1 mL) salt

⅛ tsp (0.5 mL) garlic powder

¼ tsp (1 mL) sugar

¼ tsp (1 mL) pepper

1 Tbsp canned diced mild green chilies, rinsed, drained, and dried with paper towels

¼ cup (60 mL) green onion, trimmed and finely chopped

Makes about 1 cup (250 mL).

Per 1 Tbsp (15 mL): 18 cals, 1.4 g fat, 0.2 g sat. fat, 40 mg sodium, 1 g carb, 0.2 g protein

Beverage Suggestion:
Margarita or Mexican beer

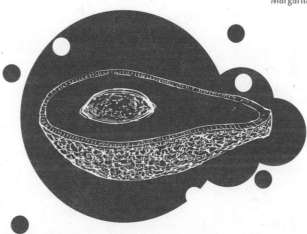

casual Crowd Pleasers

Drive-in and Diner Delights

56 Pissaladière
57 Curried Yams Fries with Cucumber Cilantro Dip
57 Cucumber Cilantro Dip
58 Double Fried French Fries
60 Pomme Frites
61 Oven Fries
62 Grilled Chicken Poutine
63 Cheddar Stuffed Beef Burgers
64 Italian Meatball Sliders
65 Hot Halibut Sliders
66 Onion Rings

Pizza and Pub-style Treats

68 Pizza Dough
70 Chorizo and Sweet Pepper Pizza
71 Smoked Salmon Pizza
72 Pork Tenderloin Nuggets with Honey Lemon Dijon Dip

Southern Specialties

73 Cajun Calamari Rings
73 Creole Seasoning
74 Debbie Fried Chicken (DFC)
76 Stoplight Chili
77 Chili Cheese Fries
78 Ginger Garlic Ribs
80 Power Crunch Chicken Wings with Spicy Barbecue Sauce
82 Salt and Pepper Cocktail Ribs
82 Salt and Pepper Chicken Wings
83 Uncle Doug's Nachos
84 Taco Beef

Pissaladière

An excellent (and economical) vegetarian appetizer pizza. The egg-bread crust is buttery, light, and well loved by all. Extra black olives will keep in an airtight plastic or glass container for up to 1 month (in their brine) in the fridge or up to 2 months (drained and rinsed) in the freezer. Try them on Uncle Doug's Nachos (p. 83).

3 cups (750 mL) flour

1½ tsp (7 mL) salt

⅓ cup (80 mL) warm water

1 Tbsp (15 mL) regular (traditional) yeast, preferably Fleischmann's

3 eggs

¼ cup plus 1½ tsp (67 mL) melted butter, cooled

vegetable oil for bowl and baking sheet

¾ cup (185 mL) Marinara Sauce (p. 87)

1 cup (250 mL) diced green pepper

1 cup (250 mL) sliced mushrooms

half a 13 oz (375 mL) can black olives, rinsed and drained well

½ cup (125 mL) grated Parmesan cheese

Makes 48 triangular pieces.

Per piece: 53 cals, 2 g fat, 1 g sat. fat, 17 mg cholesterol, 136 mg sodium, 6.8 g carbs, 1.8 g protein

Beverage Suggestion: Beaujolais, Pinot Noir, or Merlot wine; medium-dark beer

In a medium-large bowl, mix together flour and salt. In a small bowl, add yeast to warm water. Stir to combine, then let stand for 10 to 15 minutes until yeast has expanded and bubbled up. In a medium bowl, beat eggs, add melted butter, and mix in activated yeast. Make a well in the salted flour; pour in the wet ingredients. Stir the mixture until smooth and a dough forms.

Briefly knead the dough on a clean surface—sprinkle with a bit of flour if sticky. Let rise in a clean, lightly oiled bowl covered with a clean cloth or plastic wrap, until doubled in size, about 1 hour. Punch the dough down, all over the top, to expel all the air. Roll out the dough to completely fill an 11 × 17 inch (28 × 42.5 cm) oiled, rimmed baking sheet.

Avoiding ½ inch (1 cm) of outer edge, spread Marinara Sauce over crust, top with green pepper, mushrooms, and olives, then sprinkle with Parmesan cheese. Let pizza rise in a warm place until crust has puffed up and almost doubled in size, about 1 hour.

Preheat the oven to 400°F (200°C). Bake the pizza on the middle rack for 15 minutes, then reduce heat to 350°F (180°C) and bake for 15 minutes more. The crust should be firm around the edges, completely puffed in the middle, and golden all over the top.

Slice into 24 almost square pieces, then divide each one diagonally to make triangles.

Curried Yam Fries with Cucumber Cilantro Dip

Try this interesting flavour combination for something greater than ordinary!

Cut yams into long ½-inch (1.25 cm) wide slices, then make ½-inch (1.25 cm) wide fries. Place fries in a medium bowl; add 1½ tablespoons (7.5 mL) of the flour and stir to coat well.

Fill a large, deep skillet with oil at least 1 inch (2.5 cm) deep but do not exceed one-quarter of the pan's total depth. Oil level will rise when fries are added so you do not want to overfill the pan. If using a deep fryer, preheat oil according to manufacturer's directions to about 375°F (190°C) or heat oil in the skillet on medium-high until rippling but not smoking.

In a medium mixing bowl, combine the seasonings; have a pair of tongs or a wooden spoon handy.

Add remaining flour to fries and toss again to coat. Cook fries until golden and cooked through, about 3 to 4 minutes. Drain well on paper towels, then add to the seasoning bowl and mix gently to thoroughly coat with curry seasonings.

Cucumber Cilantro Dip

This light, fresh dip is a great contrast to the curry!

In a small bowl, mix together all ingredients; cover and refrigerate. This dip can be made up to 1 day ahead.

1½ lb (750 g) yams, peeled

3 Tbsp (45 mL) flour, divided

1 cup (250 mL) canola oil for deep-frying, or correct amount for your deep fryer

½ tsp (2 mL) coarse sea salt

¾ tsp (4 mL) Garam Masala seasoning (p. 113)

¼ tsp (1 mL) ground cumin

¼ tsp (1 mL) pepper

1 recipe Cucumber Cilantro Dip (p. 57)

Serves 2.

Per serving with ¼ cup (125 mL) dip: 515 cals, 16 g fat, 5.7 g sat. fat, 17 mg cholesterol, 949 mg sodium, 85.7 g carbs, 7 g protein

Beverage Suggestion:
Apple or pear cider

¼ cup (60 mL) finely diced English cucumber

⅓ cup (80 mL) sour cream

1 Tbsp (15 mL) cilantro leaves, minced

¼ tsp (1 mL) onion salt

¼ tsp (1 mL) pepper

Makes ½ cup (125 mL).

Per Tbsp (15 mL): 21 cals, 2 g fat, 4 mg cholesterol, 79 mg sodium, 0.5 g carbs, 0.3 g protein

Double Fried French Fries

This cooking method is from the Sandcastle Restaurant in Sylvan Lake, Alberta. They had the best fries for takeout to enjoy at the beach across the street! I am sorry to say that the Sandcastle no longer exists, but their fries live on!

2 lb (1 kg) red or white potatoes, unpeeled

3 cups (750 mL) canola or corn oil for deep-frying, or correct amount for your deep fryer

½ tsp (2 mL) sea salt

½ tsp (2 mL) freshly ground pepper

Serves 4.

Per serving: 320 cals, 13.9 g fat, 1.1 g sat. fat, 308 mg sodium, 43.5 g carbs, 5 g protein

Beverage Suggestion: ice cold Pepsi; light beer

Prep work

Fill a large bowl half full with cold water. Wash potatoes and cut potatoes into fries ⅓ to ½ inch (8 mm to 1 cm) wide. As you cut them, place fries in cold water to soak. When you have cut up all the potatoes and added them to the soaking water, drain the bowl and refill it again with cold water. Soak fries for at least 30 minutes total. Potatoes can be precut and soaked several hours ahead, and even up to 2 days, if covered and refrigerated. Remove fries from the fridge 30 minutes before cooking, and drain and dry them (see Cooking Tip [p. 59]).

First fry

Fill a large, deep skillet with oil at least 1 inch (2.5 cm) deep but do not exceed one-quarter of the pan's total depth. Oil level will rise when fries are added so you do not want to overfill the pan. If using a deep fryer, preheat oil according to the manufacturer's instructions to about 375°F (190°C). Divide fries into 4 equal portions. Have a medium-large baking pan, lined with paper towels, ready to hold fries as they are removed from the skillet.

Preheat oil on medium-high until rippling. Test temperature with half of a fry—it should sizzle immediately upon insertion into the oil. Fry one portion of fries at a time for 3 to 4 minutes, until cooked through but not yet browned. Test potatoes for doneness (see Cooking Tip [p. 59]).

When fries are cooked through, remove from oil and add to the paper-towel-lined pan. Repeat the process until all fries are cooked through but not browned. Unless browning fries immediately, remove skillet from heat or turn off deep fryer. After the first fry, you can keep cooked fries in a container, covered and refrigerated, for up to 1 week before the second fry.

Second fry

Remove fries from the fridge 30 minutes before frying.

Ten minutes before serving, preheat or reheat oil as for first fry. While oil is heating, line a baking pan with clean paper towels for draining fries and divide potatoes into at least 2 portions.

Once oil is at correct temperature, use heatproof tongs to carefully add fries and then spread them out to brown evenly. Do not overcrowd or fries will not be as crisp as desired. Cook fries until golden brown, about 2 to 3 minutes, then drain quickly on the paper-towel-lined tray. Sprinkle with salt and pepper to taste and cook the next batch. You can keep them warm in the oven at 200°F (95°C) but they will lose some of their crispness.

Drying potatoes: The easiest way I have found to dry potatoes after washing them is to lay out a large tea towel and spread potato pieces on top; cover with another tea towel and gently rub and toss them with the cloth until dry.

Testing potatoes for doneness: With heatproof tongs, remove and test one fry by breaking it in half to see if it is somewhat translucent. Raw potatoes appear shiny, creamy in colour, and they are crunchy or firm in the middle. You want the fries to be limp and no longer shiny. The centre should be cooked completely through. This is similar to testing pasta by breaking a piece in two to see if the centre is cooked.

Pomme Frites

The crispiest and tastiest little fries on the planet! Combine them with Mocha Chili Rubbed Steaks (p. 102) for an excellent French-bistro-style meal.

Follow the Double Fried French Fries recipe (p. 58) but cut potatoes ¼ inch (6 mm) thick. Fries will cook a little faster because they are thinner. Cook the first fry for 2 to 3 minutes and the second fry for 1 to 2 minutes, or until golden.

2 lb (1 kg) red or white potatoes, unpeeled

3 cups (750 mL) canola or corn oil for deep-frying, or correct amount for your deep fryer

½ tsp (2 mL) sea salt

½ tsp (2 mL) freshly ground pepper

Serves 4 lucky people.

Per serving: 320 cals, 13.9 g fat, 1.1 g sat. fat, 308 mg sodium, 43.5 g carbs, 5 g protein

Beverage Suggestion:
anything French

Oven Fries

A healthier version of fries but still crispy good!

Prep work

Line a baking sheet with parchment, trimming the paper to sit flat in the corners of the baking sheet.

Fill a large bowl half full with cold water. Wash potatoes and cut into fries ⅓ to ½ inch (8 mm to 1 cm) wide. As you cut them, place fries in cold water to soak. When you have cut up all the potatoes and added them to the soaking water, drain the bowl and refill it again with cold water. Soak fries for at least 30 minutes total. Potatoes can be precut and soaked several hours ahead, and even up to 2 days, if covered and refrigerated. Remove fries from the fridge 30 minutes before cooking, and drain and dry them (see Cooking Tip [p. 59]).

Baking

Preheat the oven to 425°F (220°C). Place fries in a medium bowl and drizzle them with oil, tossing gently to coat them well. Spread them out on the parchment-lined tray in a single layer. Bake for 20 to 30 minutes in the lower third of the oven. Check fries at 20 minutes and shuffle their position if the outer ones are browning quicker than the middle ones. Return to the oven for 5 to 10 minutes, more or until golden and crisp. Sprinkle fries with salt and pepper before serving.

parchment paper for baking sheet
2 lb (1 kg) red or white potatoes, unpeeled
1 Tbsp (30 mL) canola or corn oil
½ tsp (2 mL) sea salt (regular or coarse)
½ tsp (2 mL) freshly ground pepper

Serves 4.

Per serving: 227 cals, 3.7 g fat, 0.6 g sat. fat, 309 mg cholesterol, 43.6 g carbs, 5 g protein

Beverage Suggestion:
light beer

Grilled Chicken Poutine

Poutine is available with some pretty unique and tasty toppings these days. Here's one of my favourite versions for you to try—it is not as sinful as some! See Chili Cheese Fries (p. 77) for advice on serving individual portions. If you prepare the gravy, prep the fries, and cook the chicken ahead of time, this dish can be assembled immediately after you bake the fries.

vegetable oil or non-stick spray oil

8 oz (250 g) boneless and skinless chicken breast, cut into two ½-inch (1 cm) thick slices

1 recipe Oven Fries (p. 61), cooked and hot from the oven

2 cups (500 mL) Wine Gravy (p. 110) made with low-sodium chicken stock, heated

1 cup (250 mL) cheese curds, coarsely chopped, or 1½ cups (375 mL) grated cheddar cheese

parchment paper for baking sheet

Serves 4.

Per serving: 595 cals, 22.3 g fat, 11.6 g sat. fat, 100 mg cholesterol, 810 mg sodium, 53.4 g carbs, 45.4 g protein

Beverage Suggestion: Chardonnay; pale ale beer

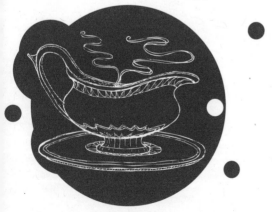

Preheat your grill to medium-high and spray it lightly with oil. Add chicken slices to the grill and cook each side for 3 to 4 minutes. Chicken should be well marked by the grill and firm to the touch when cooked through—do not overcook. Transfer grilled chicken to a heatproof bowl, cover, and let stand for at least 5 minutes before slicing. Cut chicken into ½ × 1 × ¼-inch (1 × 2.5 × 0.5 cm) thick slices. (Any juices left in the bowl can be used to thin the gravy if it is too thick.)

Preheat the broiler to 500°F (260°C) and line a baking sheet with parchment paper. Stack fries 1½ inches (4 cm) thick on the lined baking sheet. Pour gravy over the fries, top with pieces of hot chicken, and sprinkle with cheese. Broil on the second rack from the top of the oven until cheese is completely melted and starting to bubble, about 5 to 6 minutes if using curds, but only 3 to 4 minutes for grated cheese.

Cheddar Stuffed Beef Burgers

These delicious, substantial burgers are perfect for a casual backyard barbecue! Add an order of Oven Fries (p. 61) for an easy accompaniment.

Preheat your grill to medium-high. In a medium bowl, combine ground beef, onion, parsley, and seasonings; stir well. Divide into eight 2½ oz (75 g) portions and flatten onto individual waxed paper squares to make 4-inch (10 cm) patties.

Divide grated cheese into 4 portions and, with your fingers, press each one into a round cheese patty 2½ inches (6 cm) in diameter. Place 1 cheese round in the centre of 4 of the beef patties, then top each cheese round with a second beef patty. Carefully remove the top layer of waxed paper and discard. Press around outside rim of each burger stack to join the two edges and make 4 large, stuffed burger patties. Keep waxed paper sheets under stuffed patties.

Place each patty, meat side down, on the grill; carefully peel off the waxed paper sheet and discard. Grill burgers about 7 minutes per side to cook through; grill cut sides of buns until golden, about 1 minute. Spread buns with your favourite condiments, if using, before adding cooked patties and topping with vegetable garnish, if using.

Cooking Tip: Try other types of cheese, such as Jalapeno Monterey Jack for a Mexican-style burger.

1¼ lb (625 g) lean ground beef, sirloin or chuck

⅓ cup (80 mL) red or white onion, diced small

2 Tbsp (30 mL) fresh parsley leaves, minced

1 Tbsp (15 mL) Worcestershire sauce

½ tsp (2 mL) salt

½ tsp (2 mL) pepper

1 cup (250 mL) grated aged or sharp cheddar cheese

eight 5-inch (13 cm) squares waxed paper

4 Kaiser or hamburger buns, sliced

burger condiments, such as ketchup, mustard, relish, and mayo (optional)

vegetable garnishes, such as lettuce, tomato, and onion (optional)

Makes 4 burgers.

Per burger with bun (without condiments or garnish): 627 cals, 37.9 g fat, 17.3 g sat. fat, 134 mg cholesterol, 958 mg sodium, 31.3 g carbs, 39.8 g protein

Beverage Suggestion: wheat beer or medium-dark beer

Italian Meatball Sliders

Mini meatball sandwiches—a real hit with guys (and girls) at game time or anytime! Slider buns are available in the bakery section of most large grocery stores or substitute a small, 2-inch (5 cm) diameter, dinner bun.

With your fingers, remove a small amount of bread from inside the top and bottom halves of each bun to make room for a meatball. (The bread removed from the buns can chopped in a food processor for fresh breadcrumbs, or cubed for Herb Croutons [p. 19]). If you prep the buns ahead, be sure to keep them sealed in a plastic bag until you are ready to assemble the sliders so they stay fresh. Add about 1 teaspoon (5 mL) Parmesan cheese to each bun.

Spoon 1 hot meatball, coated with Marinara Sauce, into each slider bun, closing the lid over each meatball after assembling. Serve sliders immediately but save one, or better yet two, for the cook.

Serving Tip: If you are not serving all the sliders at the same time, keep meatballs warm in a slow cooker on the lowest setting. Prep the slider buns ahead of time but keep covered so they don't dry out. That way, you can easily assemble sliders as needed and serve each batch hot.

1 recipe Meatballs in Marinara Sauce (p. 86) made with only 1 cup (250 mL) sauce, hot

30 slider buns, sliced

⅔ cup (160 mL) finely grated Parmesan cheese, at room temperature

Makes 30 quickly disappearing appetizers.

Per slider: 80 cals, 3 g fat, 1.1 g sat. fat, 14 mg cholesterol, 183 mg sodium, 8.1 g carbs, 5.2 g protein

Beverage Suggestion:
Côtes-du-rhônes red wine or Chianti; lager or ale beer

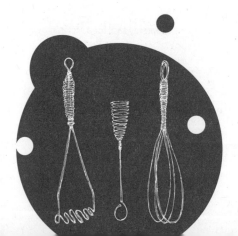

Hot Halibut Sliders

A huge hit at any party; the resulting comment is always "those are *sooooo gooood!!!*" If fresh fish is not available, frozen cod is a better choice than frozen halibut because it remains moist even after freezing.

If you are slicing the buns ahead of time, be sure to keep them sealed in a plastic bag until you are ready to assemble the sliders so they stay fresh.

Cut fish into twenty-four ½-inch (1 cm) thick pieces, about 1½ inches (4 cm) square; you may need to divide into thinner fillets first. Pieces do not have to be perfectly square; the goal is to have 24 pieces of approximately the same size that will fit the slider buns.

In a medium bowl, place about half the halibut pieces and sprinkle with 2 to 3 teaspoons (10 to 15 mL) Creole Seasoning. Stir well to coat and add another 1 teaspoon (5 mL) seasoning if more is needed to evenly coat the fish. Repeat with remaining fish portions and another 2 to 4 teaspoons (10 to 20 mL) seasoning until all the fish is seasoned.

Heat a large non-stick skillet on high for 4 to 5 minutes until very hot. Add 2 tablespoons (30 mL) of the butter and all the halibut pieces. Sear fish on high heat for 1 minute; add remaining butter and flip fish pieces to cook the other side for 1 minute. Remove pan from heat immediately and cover.

Spread buns with mayonnaise, using about ½ teaspoon (2.5 mL) per bun half. Add a piece of fish to each bun and platter the sliders, saving two for yourself. Serve immediately. (It is important to save two sliders for yourself, because once they are served to your guests, you won't see any until you make them again.)

1 lb (500 g) halibut, or substitute
2 Pacific Grey cod fillets, preferably fresh
1 recipe Creole Seasoning (p. 73)
¼ cup (60 mL) butter, divided
24 slider buns, sliced
½ cup (125 mL) whole-egg mayonnaise such as Kraft Real or Hellman's

Makes 24 sliders.

Per slider: 155 cals, 6.9 g fat, 2.1 g sat. fat, 27 mg cholesterol, 356 mg sodium, 15.7 g carbs, 7.2 g protein

Beverage Suggestion:
Chardonnay; white sangria; Corona or Dos Equis beer

Onion Rings

My brother's first choice at any drive-in or burger joint when we were teens! Try them with Cheddar Stuffed Burgers (p. 63).

1 large sweet onion, about 13 to 14 oz (405 to 435 g), top and bottom trimmed, skin discarded

1 cup (250 mL) flour

1⅓ cup (330 mL) club soda or beer

½ to ¾ cup (125 to 185 mL) Panko breadcrumbs

3 cups (750 mL) canola or corn oil for deep-frying, or correct amount for your deep fryer

salt and pepper in shakers to serve with rings

Serves 4, with about 6 rings per person.
Per serving (using club soda for batter):
279 cals, 10.1 g fat, 1.4 g sat. fat, 148 mg sodium, 40.9 g carbs, 5.9 g protein

Beverage Suggestion:
lager or ale beer; root beer

Fill a medium-large bowl with cold water. Slice peeled onion into about four ½-inch (1 cm) slices. Carefully pop inner rings apart, keeping the circles intact, and soak them in cold water for 20 to 30 minutes. (Doing so helps to remove some of the strong onion juice so they taste sweeter.) Drain rings and dry them well with a clean tea towel or paper towels.

Preheat the oven to 200ºF (95°C) to keep cooked onion rings warm while frying remaining ones. Place flour in a medium bowl, then gradually add club soda or beer, whisking to combine. Place ½ cup (125 mL) of the Panko breadcrumbs in a second medium bowl.

Fill a large, deep skillet with oil at least 1 inch (2.5 cm) deep but do not exceed one-quarter of the pan's total depth. Oil level will rise when onion rings are added so you do not want to overfill the pan. If using a deep fryer, preheat oil according to manufacturer's directions to about 375°F (190°C). Have a medium-large baking pan, lined with paper towels, ready for holding rings once cooked.

Preheat oil on medium-high until rippling. Test temperature with one end of an onion piece; it should sizzle immediately upon insertion into the oil.

One at a time, dip each onion ring in the batter, letting any excess drain back into the bowl. Next, coat each side of the battered rings with breadcrumbs. To avoid wastage, only add more breadcrumbs to the bowl as needed. Place each ring in the hot oil immediately after dipping and coating. Do not overcrowd onion rings while cooking—fry only what fits easily in the skillet or deep-fryer in a single layer with ½ inch (1 cm) spacing, ideally about a quarter of the total number of rings at a time.

Cook onion rings until golden brown, about 3 to 4 minutes. Place on prepared baking pan to drain and keep warm in the oven. Repeat process until all rings are battered and cooked. Add salt and pepper to taste.

Pizza Dough

Excellent, strong pizza dough for medium-thick crusts. I use this recipe for Chorizo and Sweet Pepper Pizza (p. 70) and Smoked Salmon Pizza (p. 71). Semolina flour gives this dough a strong, resilient nature; you can find it in the specialty flour section of most grocery stores. It is also available at most Italian delis and markets.

1¼ cups (310 mL) lukewarm water
1½ tsp (7 mL) sugar
2 Tbsp (30 mL) olive oil
¼ oz (7.5 g) package regular (traditional) yeast, or 2¼ tsp (11 mL)
1½ tsp (7 mL) salt
1 cup (250 mL) semolina flour
2 cups (500 mL) all-purpose flour
vegetable oil for bowl

Makes two 12-inch (30 cm) or four 8-inch (20 cm) pizza crusts.

Per 12-inch (30 cm) pizza crust: 876 cals, 15.6 g fat, 2.1 g sat. fat, 1771 mg sodium, 159.3 g carbs, 24.4 g protein

Per 8-inch (20 cm) crust: 436 cals, 7.8 g fat, 1 g sat. fat, 886 mg sodium, 79.7 g carbs, 12.2 g protein

Cooking Tip: Freeze the other half of the pizza dough for up to 2 weeks. Just after you punch it down, slide it into a plastic freezer bag, and place in the freezer before it rises.

Preparing

In a large bowl, or the bowl of a stand mixer with a dough hook attachment, place lukewarm water, sugar, and olive oil. Stir well to dissolve sugar. Add yeast and stir with a whisk until mixed. Let sit for 10 to 15 minutes to activate yeast; it will froth up and almost double in volume.

Add salt and all the semolina flour at once; stir well with a wooden spoon or use the stand mixer's low setting. Gradually add the all-purpose flour, 2 to 3 tablespoons (30 to 45 mL) at a time, as you continue mixing. (If not using a stand mixer, you may have to remove the dough from the bowl and work in the last bit of flour by hand.)

Place dough on a clean and dry section of kitchen counter, or use a large cutting board. To knead, sprinkle small amounts of flour on top of the dough, then fold it over and pull the sides in. Repeat kneading until the dough is smooth and no longer sticky.

Oil a large bowl and add the dough. Cover with a clean cloth or plastic wrap and let rise for 1 hour, or until doubled in size.

Punch dough down several times with your fist to get rid of any air bubbles. Divide dough into two equal portions for two 12-inch (30 cm) pizzas, or into four portions for 8-inch (20 cm) pizzas. If you are making the dough a few hours ahead, wrap each piece in plastic wrap or place in a plastic bag and refrigerate until 30 minutes before rolling out and topping.

Baking

Press or roll out the dough portions to match your pan size. If using a pizza stone, sprinkle your work surface liberally with all-purpose flour, cornmeal, or semolina flour to prevent crust from sticking to the stone once you transfer it. Preheat the stone according to the manufacturer's instructions; check recommended time for preheating as it may take 1 hour.

Preheat the oven to 450°F (240°C), or your oven's maximum temperature. You can oil the pizza pans with a little olive oil but do it lightly. Top pizzas with desired toppings and let rise for 15 to 20 minutes before baking. Bake for 15 to 20 minutes, or until crust is golden and crisp in the middle. Cool for 3 to 4 minutes before cutting so the cheese sets a little.

Chorizo and Sweet Pepper Pizza

Sausage and peppers go together so well, and luckily they are always available to satisfy that pizza craving. Chorizo is a spicy Spanish pork sausage.

½ recipe Pizza Dough (p. 68), or substitute a 12-inch (30 cm) purchased pizza crust

1 Tbsp (15 mL) vegetable oil

1 lb (500 g) chorizo sausages, casings removed

1½ cups (375 mL) diced onion (1 medium)

¾ to 1 cup (185 to 250 mL) Marinara Sauce (p. 87)

2 cups (500 mL) sliced red, yellow, or orange bell pepper (1 large or 2 small)

½ cup (125 mL) feta cheese, rinsed well, dried, and crumbled

2 cups (500 mL) grated Edam, Monterey Jack, or Mozzarella cheese

2 Tbsp (30 mL) fresh parsley leaves, minced

Makes one 12-inch (30 cm) pizza with 8 large, tasty wedges.

Per piece: 416 cals, 24.1 g fat, 10.1 g sat. fat, 61 mg cholesterol, 1117 mg sodium, 28.9 g carbs, 20.8 g protein

Beverage Suggestion: Shiraz, Zinfandel, or Malbec wine

Cooking Tip: You can substitute hot Italian sausage for the chorizo if you prefer it.

Line a baking dish or plate with paper towels for draining sausage meat after cooking. In a medium-large skillet, heat oil on medium-high. Crumble sausage meat into the skillet with onion. Cook, stirring frequently to break up the sausage mixture, until meat is no longer pink in the middle, about 7 to 10 minutes. You want the meat lightly browned and the onions cooked until transparent or light golden. (If mixture is browning too quickly, turn the heat down to medium.) Drain mixture well in the prepared pan and set aside to cool.

Cut pepper(s) open; remove stem and pith and discard. Cut into ¼-inch (6 mm) slices, then cut all the slices in half.

Preheat the oven to 450°F (240°C). Lightly oil a 12-inch (30 cm) round pizza pan. Press out the dough according to the instructions given in the Pizza Dough recipe (p. 68). Place the crust on the prepared pizza pan. Spread with Marinara Sauce, avoiding ½ inch (1 cm) of outer edge. Distribute cooked sausage mixture evenly overtop, then add pepper slices. Sprinkle with feta and top pizza with an even cover of grated cheese; finish with parsley.

Bake pizza for 25 minutes in the lower third of the oven, rotating halfway through. If using a precooked pizza crust, reduce cooking time to 15 to 18 minutes. Pizza is done when crust is golden and cheese is bubbling.

Smoked Salmon Pizza

Cream cheese makes this pizza an extra-special treat for smoked salmon lovers. It was always a sellout at Decadence Café whenever it was the daily pizza special and makes a great appetizer pizza for parties. Lox-style smoked salmon is sometimes labelled as "cold-smoked."

In a medium bowl, use a wooden spoon to thoroughly mix cream cheese with seasoning, dill, and onion. Separate salmon slices and cut into ½-inch (1 cm) pieces. Press or roll out Pizza Dough to make four 8-inch (20 cm) crusts and place them onto 2 lightly oiled baking sheets or use 4 small pizza pans.

Spread each crust with one-quarter of the cream cheese mixture and top with one-quarter of the smoked salmon pieces. Evenly divide the grated cheese among the pizzas, making sure to cover all the salmon pieces, and then top with parsley. Let pizzas rise in a warm place for 30 to 40 minutes, or until puffed up.

Preheat the oven to 450°F (240°C). Bake pizzas in the middle of the oven for 15 to 20 minutes, or until golden and firm on the bottom and top. If baking 4 small pizzas at the same time, you may need to rotate the pans halfway through the baking time. If you are baking pizzas on large baking sheets, place one on the third rack down and the other on the fourth rack; switch them halfway through baking, though they may need 5 minutes more to crisp the bottoms.

Let pizzas cool for 5 minutes before slicing. Cut each pizza into 8 wedges.

11 oz (330 g) regular or light block cream cheese, at room temperature

¼ tsp (1 mL) salt

¼ tsp (1 mL) pepper

¼ tsp (1 mL) dried dillweed

⅔ cup (160 mL) diced red onion

1 recipe Pizza Dough (p. 68), divided into 4 equal portions

7 oz (200 g) sliced lox-style smoked salmon

3 cups (750 mL) grated Edam or Monterey Jack cheese

1 Tbsp (15 mL) minced fresh parsley leaves or dried parsley flakes

Makes 32 appetizer wedges.

Per wedge: 137 cals, 8.1 g fat, 4 g sat. fat, 21 mg cholesterol, 372 mg sodium, 10.4 g carbs, 5.9 g protein

Beverage Suggestion: Riesling or Viognier wine

Pork Tenderloin Nuggets with Honey Lemon Dijon Dip

These are the ultimate nugget-style treat, especially for us grown-ups. This recipe makes about 36 nuggets; some will be quite small and others will be large. Three or four of the larger ones—or five or six nuggets, if they are assorted sizes—constitutes a medium portion.

2 pork tenderloins, about 2 to 2½ lb (1 to 1.25 kg), trimmed and any skin removed

salt and pepper in shakers or grinders

½ cup (125 mL) flour, divided

2 large eggs

1½ to 2 cups (375 to 500 mL) Panko breadcrumbs, in a medium bowl

1 cup (250 mL) canola oil for frying

1 recipe Honey Lemon Dijon Dip (p. 45)

Makes about 36 nuggets.

Per nugget with 1½ tsp (7.5 mL) dip: 158 cals, 12 g fat, 1.5 g sat. fat, 32 mg cholesterol, 185 mg sodium, 5.9 g carbs, 6.5 g protein

Beverage Suggestion:
Riesling or Viognier wine

Prep work

Slice pork tenderloins into ½-inch (1 cm) thick medallions. Sprinkle both sides of pork pieces with salt and pepper. In a medium bowl, toss half of the pork with ¼ cup (60 mL) of the flour; stir to coat well. Transfer dredged pork pieces to a plate and repeat procedure with the rest of the pork and flour. Place eggs in a medium bowl and whisk well to incorporate the yolks into the whites.

Working in small batches, thoroughly coat pork pieces with egg, letting any extra drain back into the bowl, then coat pieces completely with breadcrumbs. Set breaded pieces on a plate and refrigerate, uncovered, for at least 30 minutes before frying.

Frying and serving

Line a baking pan or baking sheet with paper towels for draining pork nuggets after frying. In a large non-stick skillet, heat oil on medium-high to 375°F (190°C), or until rippling but not smoking. Fry batches of pork nuggets until dark golden and crisp, about 2 to 3 minutes per side. Cook nuggets in two or three batches—do not crowd them too much or the sides will not be crispy. Drain cooked nuggets on the paper-towel-lined pan. Repeat process until all nuggets are cooked. Serve with Honey Lemon Dijon Dip on the side.

Cajun Calamari Rings

Spicy with a light, crispy coating. One of my friend Nick's favourites!

In a medium bowl, sprinkle squid rings with Creole Seasoning and stir well to coat evenly. They should be somewhat moist—if not, let stand for 5 minutes. Add 3 tablespoons (45 mL) rice flour and mix well to coat. Let stand for 10 minutes while you preheat the oil in a large non-stick skillet on medium-high to 375°F (190°C), or until rippling but not smoking. Have a baking tray lined with paper towels ready for draining them. Add 1 tablespoon (15 mL) more flour to the bowl containing the squid rings and stir to coat again. Gently shake off any excess flour, then add about half the rings to the hot oil.

Cook squid rings for 1 minute to brown the flour, then turn them quickly and cook for 1 minute more. They should go from translucent to white very quickly—do not overcook or they will be tough and chewy. Drain on the paper-towel-lined tray and serve immediately.

Cooking Tip: The size of calamari rings can vary; a 10-ounce (300-gram) package of medium ones usually contains four to five dozen.

Creole Seasoning

This is an excellent seasoning for blackened fish!

In a small bowl, mix all ingredients together to combine thoroughly; store in an airtight container.

10 oz (300 g) calamari squid rings (about 50 to 60 rings), thawed if frozen, rinsed, and dried

2½ tsp (12 mL) Creole Seasoning (p. 73)

¼ cup (60 mL) white rice flour, divided

1½ cups (375 mL) canola oil for deep-frying

Per calamari ring (based on 0.2 oz [6 g] each): 17 cals, 1.2 g fat, 0.1 g sat. fat, 13 mg cholesterol, 26 mg sodium, 0.8 g carbs, 0.9 g protein

Beverage Suggestion:
Sauvignon Blanc, Fumé Blanc, or Pinot Gris wine

1½ tsp (7 mL) black pepper

1 Tbsp plus 1 tsp (20 mL) paprika, sifted if lumpy

1½ tsp (7 mL) garlic salt

1½ tsp (7 mL) table salt

1½ tsp (7 mL) onion powder

1½ tsp (7 mL) oregano

½ tsp (2 mL) ground thyme

½ tsp (2 mL) cayenne pepper (or more if desired)

Makes 5 Tbsp (75 mL).

Per Tbsp (15 mL): 13 cals, 0.2 g fat, 1416 mg sodium, 2.2 g carbs, 0.5 g protein

Debbie Fried Chicken (DFC)

My version of a Southern classic—I hope you enjoy it! Start making it the day before so the chicken can marinate. You can make extra for the freezer (see tip on p. 75) but good luck with that: I have a friend who once took leftover fried chicken with him on a flight from Victoria to Phoenix because he just couldn't leave it behind. (*Hi Chuck!*)

2½ to 3 lb (1.25 to 1.5 kg) chicken pieces (about 12), skin on and bone in

2 Tbsp (30 mL) salt, divided

1 large onion, sliced ¼ inch (6 mm) thick, rings or half rounds, divided

4 cups (1 L) buttermilk, divided

Breading

1½ cups (375 mL) flour

1 tsp (5 mL) paprika, sifted

1 tsp (5 mL) oregano

½ tsp (2 mL) salt

½ tsp (2 mL) pepper

¼ tsp (1 mL) onion powder

¼ tsp (1 mL) garlic powder

3 cups (750 mL) canola oil for deep-frying, divided

Makes about 12 pieces, enough to serve 3 or 4 people.

Per piece: 308 cals, 19.4 g fat, 5.1 g sat. fat, 78 mg cholesterol, 280 mg sodium, 12.6 g carbs, 21.2 g protein

Beverage Suggestion: pale ale or lager beer; iced tea

Brining and marinating

Place chicken pieces in a large bowl and sprinkle with about 1½ teaspoons (7 mL) of the salt; stir well. Repeat procedure until you have used up all the salt and chicken is evenly coated. Cover and refrigerate for 2½ to 3 hours.

Place chicken in a large colander in the sink and thoroughly rinse off the salt with cold water; rinse 3 or 4 times to be sure to remove all the salt you can. Pick a container that is glass, plastic, or stainless steel that can fit all the chicken, onion, and buttermilk. Add one-quarter of the onions and then cover them with one-third of the chicken, followed by ½ to 1 cup (125 to 250 mL) buttermilk. Continue layering onions, chicken, and buttermilk until all of the onions and chicken are used and completely coated with buttermilk. If your container is compact, you may only need 3 cups (750 mL) of buttermilk—if it is larger, you will need all of it. Cover and refrigerate overnight, or for at least 8 hours.

Breading and cooking

Have a platter or tray available to put the chicken pieces on. Mix flour and seasonings together in a medium bowl; stir well. Drain the buttermilk off the chicken and discard the buttermilk and onions. Dredge each piece of chicken in the flour mixture and coat thoroughly; set aside on the platter while you coat the other pieces.

Do not discard flour after breading. Let breaded chicken sit for 10 minutes; the pieces will get sticky and the coating will be gummy.

Preheat the oven to 375°F (190°C) and ready a shallow baking pan or tray that can fit all the chicken pieces. Pour 2 cups (500 mL) oil into a large non-stick skillet and 1 cup (250 mL) into a medium non-stick skillet. (If you don't have two skillets, you can fry chicken in two separate batches.) Preheat the oil to 375°F (190°C) on medium-high until rippling but not smoking. Return chicken pieces to the flour and thoroughly coat a second time so they are no longer sticky. Fry the chicken in the oil until golden, and then flip over to brown the other side, about 7 to 8 minutes per side. A large skillet will fit hold about 6 pieces of chicken while a medium skillet will hold about 4 pieces.

Drain fried chicken, place pieces on the baking pan, and bake for 20 to 30 minutes in the middle of the oven to finish cooking. Test doneness with a meat thermometer or poke with a skewer to see if juices run clear. For the chicken to be cooked through, it should reach an internal temperature of 185°F (85°C). Large pieces of chicken may take up to 30 minutes while wings usually take just 20 minutes.

Chicken can be kept warm in the oven for 10 to 15 minutes by dropping the temperature to 300°F (150°C) but pieces will be less crunchy.

Cooking Tip: You can double or triple this recipe because cooked chicken freezes well for up to 2 months. Served cold, DFC makes a great picnic item paired with Warm Potato Salad (p. 98).

Safe deep-frying: Always use a splatter screen when deep-frying foods in a skillet. They can be purchased at department stores and kitchen shops and usually come in medium and large sizes to fit 10-inch (25 cm) and 12-inch (30 cm) skillets, respectively. The screens help you to avoid splatter burns and help to keep your stove somewhat clean.

When removing cooked foods from hot oil, use either a strong pair of tongs that grip well or a curved strainer spoon or skimmer. Make sure your hands are clean and dry so you have a firm grip. Deep fryers come with cooking baskets that stay in the fryer while the food is being cooked; they are easy to use to when placing the food in the oil or removing and draining the food. All tools and baskets must be heatproof; if you are using a non-stick skillet, select tools that will not scratch its surface.

Stoplight Chili

Appropriately named after the colourful green, amber, and red vegetable ingredients. Double or triple the recipe so you can freeze some or make Chili Cheese Fries (p. 77) with the leftovers.

2 Tbsp (30 mL) olive oil

1 lb (500 g) ground pork, veal, chicken thigh, or turkey thigh

1 small onion, trimmed, peeled, and diced

1 medium green pepper, diced

1 medium orange pepper, diced

10 oz (300 g) mushrooms, sliced

1 tsp (5 mL) garlic, puréed or minced

14 oz (398 mL) can black beans, rinsed and drained

28 oz (796 mL) can diced tomatoes with juice

2 Tbsp (30 mL) chili powder

1 tsp (5 mL) ground cumin

¾ tsp (4 mL) salt

½ tsp (2 mL) pepper

1 Tbsp (15 mL) sugar

2 tsp (10 mL) lime juice

2 Tbsp (30 mL) minced fresh parsley leaves or dried parsley flakes

Makes 7 cups (1.75 L).

Per 1 cup (250 mL): 280 cals, 9.4 g fat, 2.5 g sat. fat, 53 mg cholesterol, 91 mg sodium, 28.6 g carbs, 20.4 g protein

Beverage Suggestion: medium to dark beer; lime margarita

Preheat the oven to 350°F (180°C) and ready a large, deep covered casserole dish or small roaster. In a large non-stick skillet, heat oil on medium-high for 1 minute. Add meat, onion, and peppers. Cook, stirring occasionally, until meat is no longer pink and vegetables have softened, about 5 to 7 minutes. Add mushrooms and garlic; cover and cook for 5 more minutes until mushrooms are soft. Add tomatoes, beans, and seasoning; stir well.

Transfer chili to the casserole dish, cover, and bake for 1 hour, stirring every 20 minutes. If chili is boiling rapidly when removed from the oven for stirring, reduce heat to 325°F (160°C). After 60 minutes, uncover chili, and continue cooking for 30 minutes more.

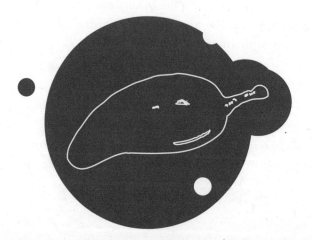

Chili Cheese Fries

Move over poutine, here's some serious competition! This is my reproduction of a dish that Doug and I shared with some friends at a pub in Friday Harbor on San Juan Island in the early 1990s. It was a very memorable treat, and I hope it will be for you as well. If you make the chili ahead of time, do the first fry of the French fries, and have the cheese measured out, you can finish this dish in about 20 minutes. The last-minute work will be a second fry of the fries, some minor assembly, and broiling to serve.

Preheat the broiler to 500°F (260°C) and line a baking sheet with parchment paper. Stack hot fries 1½ inches (4 cm) thick on the lined baking sheet. Spoon hot chili overtop fries and top with cheese. Broil on second rack from top of oven until cheese is completely melted and starts to bubble, about 3 or 4 minutes.

Cooking Tip: For easy serving, lift one side of the parchment paper onto one end of a serving platter and slide the Chili Cheese Fries off the paper and onto the plate; serve with tongs and a serving spoon. For individual servings, cut 4 pieces of parchment to fit the baking sheet. Place one-quarter of the fries on each piece of parchment, topping with ¾ cup (185 mL) chili and ½ cup (125 mL) cheese per serving.

parchment paper for baking sheet

1 recipe Double Fried French Fries (p. 58) or Oven Fries (p. 61), salt and pepper omitted

3 cups (750 mL) Stoplight Chili (p. 76), hot

2 cups (500 mL) grated sharp or aged cheddar, at room temperature

Serves 4.

Per serving, made with Double Fried French Fries: 795 cals, 42.8 g fat, 16.9 g sat. fat, 109 mg cholesterol, 492 mg sodium, 65.8 g carbs, 36.7 g protein

Per serving, made with Oven Fries: 703 cals, 32.6 g fat, 16.4 g sat. fat, 109 mg cholesterol, 492 mg sodium, 65.9 g carbs, 36.7 g protein

Beverage Suggestion: Mexican beer, such as Corona or Dos Equis

Ginger Garlic Ribs

Definitely finger-licking good so put out finger bowls and large serviettes! Hoisin sauce is available in the Asian section of most grocery stores. This glaze is also fantastic on salmon or chicken.

Ribs

2 large racks baby back pork ribs, about 2½ to 3 lb (1.25 to 1.5 kg), at room temperature

vegetable oil or parchment paper for baking sheet

Ginger Garlic Glaze

4 cups (1 L) orange juice

1 Tbsp (15 mL) minced garlic

1 Tbsp (15 mL) minced ginger

1 tsp (5 mL) crushed red chilies

1 cup (250 mL) Hoisin sauce

½ cup (125 mL) honey

2 Tbsp (30 mL) dried chives or ¼ cup (60 mL) fresh chives, snipped very small

Serves 4.

Per quarter-rack glazed ribs: 1023 cals, 68.4 g fat, 24.9 g sat. fat, 230 mg cholesterol, 835 mg sodium, 53.6 g carbs, 48.2 g protein

Per ¼ cup (60 mL) glaze: 132 cals, 0.9 g fat, 0.1 g sat. fat, 346 mg sodium, 29.6 g carbs, 1.3 g protein

Beverage Suggestion: Japanese beer or sake

Braising the ribs

Preheat the oven to 350°F (180°C). Fill a covered roaster or large casserole dish with a lid, half full with hot water. Cut racks into smaller sections, 2 to 3 ribs each, using a sharp knife to slice down between the ribs to completely separate them. Cut each rack into at least 4 pieces and place rib sections in the roaster—you want the hot water to almost cover the ribs completely. Add more hot water if needed but the roaster should be no more than three-quarters full. Cover and cook for 45 minutes.

Remove ribs from the oven, stir, replace the lid, and continue cooking for 45 more minutes. If the rib water was boiling rapidly, turn the heat down to 325°F (160°C). After 90 minutes, check ribs for tenderness; the meat should easily pull away with a fork. If you are not sure, cut off a small piece of rib meat and eat it. The meat should be very tender—if not, return ribs to the oven for another 15 to 30 minutes. (If ribs were cold when they went in the oven, they will take about 30 minutes longer to cook than room-temperature ribs.) When ribs are finished cooking, carefully remove from the water with a slotted spoon or tongs and set aside to cool in a heatproof bowl or on a plate.

Making the glaze

In a large, deep saucepan, bring orange juice to a rolling boil and cook until reduced to one-quarter original volume, about 15 to 20 minutes. Reduce heat to medium, add garlic, ginger, and chilies, and cook for 2 to 3 minutes. Add Hoisin sauce, honey, and chives; stir well. Simmer glaze for 15 to 20 minutes, stirring occasionally until thickened and syrupy.

Finishing

Preheat the broiler to 500°F (260°C) and lightly oil a baking sheet or line with parchment paper. Place all the ribs curved side down (skin side up) on the baking sheet and lightly brush top side with glaze. Broil for 4 to 5 minutes, until glaze is bubbling and ribs are lightly browned on top. Flip ribs over and liberally brush the curved, meaty side with glaze. It will take all the glaze to thoroughly coat both racks of ribs. Broil ribs for 4 to 5 minutes more, until glaze is bubbling and this side has also lightly browned.

Power Crunch Chicken Wings with Spicy Barbecue Sauce

A tangy, spicy glaze coats these incredibly tasty wings, which pack a powerful crunch!

Wings

3 cups (750 mL) canola or corn oil for deep-frying, or correct amount for your deep fryer

2¼ lb (1 kg) split chicken wings, wing tips removed

⅔ cup (160 mL) flour

1 Tbsp (15 mL) cornstarch

Makes 24 pieces.

Per piece with 2 tsp (10 mL) sauce: 136 cals, 8.5 g fat, 2 g sat. fat, 32 mg cholesterol, 90 mg sodium, 6.6 g carbs, 8.3 g protein

Beverage Suggestion: Mexican beer

First fry

Pour the oil into a large, heavy pot that is at least 4 inches deep—oil should be at least 1 inch (2.5 cm) deep but no more than one-quarter of the pot's total depth. (Oil will bubble up when wings are added so this precaution prevents any overflow.)

Heat the oil on medium-high until rippling but not smoking. Test the oil temperature with a bit of the batter if unsure—it should bubble immediately when added to the oil. If using a deep fryer, pre-heat oil to 375°F (190°C) according to the manufacturer's directions.

In a medium-large bowl, combine flour and cornstarch; stir well to mix. Add ⅔ cup (160 mL) cold water and whisk to combine until smooth. Add chicken wings and toss them with a spoon to coat well with batter.

Line a large baking pan with paper towels for draining wings after the first fry. Add wings individually to the oil so they do not stick together. Do not overcrowd them; deep-fry wings in 2 to 3 batches and cook each batch for 8 minutes. Drain well on the paper-towel-lined baking pan. Note: Wings will not be cooked through. Cool, cover, and refrigerate. You can make the wings to this point up to 1 day ahead; remove from fridge 30 minutes before second frying.

Spicy barbecue sauce

In a medium bowl, whisk together all the ingredients until combined. You can prepare this sauce up to 3 days ahead; keep covered in the fridge and bring to room temperature 30 minutes before serving.

Second fry and sauce toss

Place sauce in a large bowl for tossing. As per instructions for first fry, preheat the oil in your pot or deep fryer to 375°F (190°C) if you did the first fry ahead of time. Fry wings in 2 to 3 batches, cooking medium wings for 4 minutes. If using large wings, cook for an additional 2 to 3 minutes. Check wings for doneness by poking with a skewer—juices should run clear. Drain wings on paper towels and set aside until all wings have been fried. Just before serving, place all wings in the bowl with the sauce; toss several times to coat well. Serve immediately.

Spicy Barbecue Sauce

2 Tbsp (30 mL) soy sauce
2 Tbsp (30 mL) white vinegar or rice vinegar
½ cup (125 mL) ketchup
3 Tbsp (45 mL) honey
1 Tbsp (15 mL) Chinese chili-garlic sauce
½ tsp (2 mL) minced garlic (½ clove)
1 tsp (5 mL) minced ginger

Makes 1 cup (250 mL).

Per 1 Tbsp (15 mL): 16 cals, 5 9 mg sodium, 3.7 g carbs, 0.2 g protein

Salt and Pepper Cocktail Ribs

Way too good! You need to precook the ribs so start this recipe earlier in the day (or the day before) for an easy finish. Have the butcher cut the rack into three rows of button ribs (sweet and sour cut).

Ribs

1 large precut rack of baby back pork ribs, about 1¼ to 1½ lb (625 to 750 g)

2 Tbsp (30 mL) olive oil

Salt and Pepper Rub

1½ tsp (7 mL) salt

½ tsp (2 mL) ground Szechuan pepper

½ tsp (2 mL) ground black pepper

1 tsp (5 mL) Chinese five-spice powder

Makes 36 pieces.

Per piece: 60 cals, 5.2 g fat, 1.8 g sat. fat, 15 mg cholesterol, 112 mg sodium, 3.2 g protein

Chicken Wings

1 recipe Salt and Pepper Rub

3 lb (750 g) split chicken wings (wing tips removed), washed and dried

Makes 36 pieces.

Per piece: 89 cals, 6.8 g fat, 1.6 g sat. fat, 29 mg cholesterol, 126 mg sodium, 6.9 g protein

Beverage Suggestion: light beer; Caesar or Bloody Mary

Preheat the oven to 350°F (175°C). Place ribs in a medium roaster, with a lid, and fill three-quarters full with hot water; ribs should be submerged. Bake ribs, covered, for 90 minutes to tenderize. Check ribs every 30 minutes; if water starts boiling, reduce heat to 325°F (160°C). Drain well, and then cool, cover, and refrigerate while you prepare the rub. You can make ribs to this point up to 2 days ahead.

In a small bowl, mix spices together; use immediately or store in an airtight container for up to 3 months.

Remove ribs from the fridge 30 minutes before cooking them and preheat the oven to 350°F (175°F). In a medium bowl, gently toss ribs in olive oil, and then gradually sprinkle with seasoning while stirring them with a spoon to evenly distribute the rub. Place ribs in a large, oiled baking pan and spread them out in a single layer. Bake for 15 minutes, then flip over and bake for another 15 minutes, until lightly browned and heated through.

Salt and Pepper Chicken Wings

Preheat the oven to 400°F (200°C) and oil a large, shallow baking pan. Oil and season wings as for ribs. Place baking pan in bottom third of the oven and bake for 20 minutes. Flip each wing piece over and bake for another 20 to 25 minutes until golden.

Uncle Doug's Nachos

These nachos are loaded with great toppings; customize yours by using the ones you like most. Nachos have so much flavour that you may not want or need the salsa and sour cream.

Preheat the oven to 400°F (200°C) and lightly oil a baking sheet or pizza pan. Spread out one-third of the chips in the middle of the pan. Sprinkle chips with ½ cup (125 mL) of the cheese, distributing it evenly so each of the chips has some cheese on it. (There is nothing worse than seeing those poor plain chips when you get to the bottom; they always get discarded at the side of the plate because nobody wants them.) Top the cheese layer with one-third of each of the toppings: green onions, olives, tomatoes, jalapenos, beef. Layer one-third of the chips overtop of this layer. Repeat layering process until all chips and toppings are used up.

Bake nachos in the middle of the oven for 15 minutes, or until the cheese is bubbling and toppings are heated through. If the ingredients were cold when placed on the chips, bake for 20 minutes, and then check to see if the cheese is melted throughout. Serve with salsa and sour cream, if desired.

vegetable oil or non-stick spray oil for pan

3 oz (90 g) salted corn tortilla chips, preferably Tostitos brand, divided

1½ cups (375 mL) grated sharp or aged cheddar cheese, divided

3 Tbsp (45 mL) green onions, trimmed and chopped

3 Tbsp (45 mL) sliced black olives, rinsed and drained well

⅓ cup (80 mL) diced roma or beefsteak tomato

2 Tbsp (30 mL) sliced jalapeno pepper, stem removed

1 cup (250 mL) Taco Beef (p. 84)

1 cup (250 mL) Fresh Salsa (p. 127) or substitute purchased deli-style salsa (optional)

½ cup (125 mL) sour cream (optional)

Serves 3 as an appetizer.

Per serving (without condiments): 574 cals, 41 g fat, 19.2 g sat. fat, 108 mg cholesterol, 681 mg sodium, 22.1 g carbs, 29.3 g protein

Beverage Suggestion:
Mexican beer; lime margarita or sangria

Taco Beef

This is the recipe for the seasoned beef used in Uncle Doug's Nachos (p. 83) but it will fill 8 tacos if you use ⅓ cup (80 mL) for each one. If you prefer it hotter, add more cayenne pepper to taste. You can also use regular ground beef (see Cooking Tip).

Heat oil in a large non-stick skillet on medium-high. Add ground beef followed by the seasoning; mix well. Cook for 8 to 10 minutes, or until beef is lightly browned and no longer pink. Turn meat as it cooks, breaking up any clumps so pieces will be bite-size. Remove from heat.

Cooking Tip: If you use regular instead of lean or extra-lean ground beef, cook the meat until no longer pink but not yet brown, and then drain it well. Place half-cooked beef back in the pan with the seasonings and cook for a few more minutes to lightly brown and finish it.

2 tsp (10 mL) vegetable oil or non-stick spray oil for skillet

1 lb (500 g) lean or extra-lean ground beef, crumbled

½ tsp (2 mL) minced garlic

1 tsp (5 mL) lime juice

1 Tbsp (15 mL) chili powder

1 tsp (5 mL) ground cumin

1½ tsp (7 mL) sugar

½ tsp (2 mL) salt

¼ tsp (1 mL) pepper

⅛ tsp (0.5 mL) cayenne pepper

Makes 2¾ cups (685 mL).

Per ⅓ cup (80 mL): 148 cals, 11.1 g fat, 4 g sat. fat, 40 mg cholesterol, 46 mg sodium, 1.6 g carbs. 10.7 g protein

Beverage Suggestion:
Mexican beer; lime margarita or sangria

Family Favourites

86 Spaghettini with Meatballs and Marinara Sauce

87 Marinara Sauce

88 Baked Penne with Bolognese Sauce

90 Linguine with Red Clam Sauce

91 Classic Spaghetti Carbonara

92 Stuffed Mac and Cheese

94 Chicken with Jalapeno and Lime

95 Grilled Corn with Chili Lime Butter

96 Texan Flank Steak

98 Warm Potato Salad with Lemon Dijon Mayonnaise

99 Halibut au Gratin

100 Zucchini Lace Fritters

101 Candied Beef Tenderloin with Balsamic Butter

102 Mocha Chili Rubbed Steaks

103 Mocha Chili Rub

104 Hot Potatoes

105 Potato Chip Gratin

106 Tempura Fish with Lemon Caper Sauce

107 Lemon Caper Sauce

108 Fish and Chips

109 Prime Rib Roast with Red Wine Gravy

110 Wine Gravy

Spaghettini with Meatballs and Marinara Sauce

Who doesn't love twirling pasta and sauce splatters? This is a dish requiring bib-style serviettes. The meat mixture is very tender and less dense than ground beef. This recipe calls for half a batch of Marinara Sauce (p. 87); use the remainder for Chorizo and Sweet Pepper Pizza (p. 70).

In a medium-large bowl, mix ground meat with onion, salt, and pepper. Wash your hands well and then use them to make small meatballs, about 1 inch (2.5 cm) in diameter. Dredge meatballs in flour, shaking off any excess; set aside on a plate. Wash your hands again.

In a large non-stick skillet, heat 2 tablespoons (30 mL) oil on medium-high. Cover and fry meatballs until golden, about 3 to 4 minutes per side. Cook in several batches if necessary. If you cook meatballs with the lid on for the first 3 to 4 minutes, they will cook through and won't break when turned. Remove meatballs from the skillet and set aside on a plate.

In a medium saucepan, cook Marinara Sauce on medium heat until steaming hot; add meatballs and stir to combine. After about 4 to 5 minutes, when mixture is completely hot, reduce heat to a simmer to keep warm until pasta is cooked.

Fill a large stockpot three-quarters full of water; add salt and heat to boiling point on high. Add pasta; stir with a pasta fork to prevent sticking. Boil, stirring occasionally, until pasta is *al dente*, or cooked to your preferred tenderness. Follow package instructions and use recommended cooking time. Drain pasta and rinse with very hot water to wash off salt. Immediately divide pasta among 4 plates and top each portion with one-quarter of the meatballs and Marinara Sauce.

1 lb (500 g) lean ground veal or ground pork
¼ cup (60 mL) minced onion
½ tsp (2 mL) salt
¼ tsp (1 mL) pepper
½ cup (125 mL) flour, in a small bowl
2 Tbsp (30 mL) vegetable oil for frying
3 cups (750 mL) Marinara Sauce (p. 87)
1 lb (500 g) dried spaghettini
1 Tbsp (15 mL) salt for pasta water

Makes 4 large servings.
Per serving: 298 cals, 11.6 g fat, 3.4 g sat. fat,
92 mg cholesterol, 1324 mg sodium,
23 g carbs, 25.2 g protein

Beverage Suggestion:
dry, robust red wine, such as
Shiraz, Zinfandel, or Malbec;
medium-dark beer

Marinara Sauce

This easy tomato sauce makes a wonderful pizza or pasta sauce because it is thick and spicy!

In a large, deep saucepan or stockpot, on medium-high heat, cook onion in 1 cup (250 mL) water until transparent, about 8 to 10 minutes. Add tomato sauce and seasonings; bring sauce to a boil.

In a medium bowl, whisk together tomato paste with 1 cup (250 mL) water. Add to the pot and mix well with a wooden spoon. Bring the mixture to a boil, reduce the heat to medium-low and cook for 30 to 45 minutes, stirring occasionally. If it continues to boil rapidly, reduce heat to low. You want the sauce to bubble slowly for at least 30 minutes to blend the flavours. Stir the mixture about every 10 minutes. Remove from heat to cool.

Cooking Tip: This sauce can be thinned with a little water if it is too thick for serving on pasta. It also freezes well.

1 1/3 cups (330 mL) minced onion (1 medium onion)

28 oz can (796 mL) tomato sauce

2 Tbsp (30 mL) minced fresh parsley leaves or substitute dried parsley flakes

1/2 tsp (2 mL) cayenne pepper

1/2 tsp (2 mL) ground black pepper

1 tsp (5 mL) salt

1 tsp (5 mL) dry mustard

1 Tbsp (15 mL) Worcestershire sauce

2 tsp (10 mL) minced garlic (about 2 cloves)

1 Tbsp (15 mL) lemon juice

2 Tbsp (30 mL) sugar

1 Tbsp (15 mL) dried oregano leaves

5.5 oz (156 mL) can tomato paste

Makes 6 cups (1.5 L).

Per 1/2 cup (125 mL): 56 cals, 0.3 g fat, 624 mg sodium, 11.6 g carbs, 1.7 g protein

Beverage Suggestion:
Full-bodied, dry red wine, such as Cabernet Sauvignon or Bordeaux

Baked Penne with Bolognese Sauce

An easy, versatile sauce that is great served on pasta or layered in lasagna. Traditional Bolognese is made with veal but ground pork also yields a good result. For Baked Penne, buy a 1 lb (500 g) block of Edam cheese to melt overtop.

Sauce

In a large stockpot, cook olive oil and onions on medium-high heat for 1 to 2 minutes to sweat the onions. Add veal, crumbling the meat as you add it to the pot; stir well to mix with oil and onion. Cook for about 10 minutes, stirring frequently, until veal is no longer pink; do not brown the meat.

In a medium-large bowl, whisk together tomato paste and vegetable stock; add it to the meat along with carrot pieces and seasonings. Stir well and cook for 15 minutes to heat through and bring sauce to a gentle boil. Stir again, and then reduce heat to medium and cook, uncovered, for 1 hour, stirring every 15 minutes to prevent sticking. You can gradually reduce the heat further over the hour but maintain a low boil or gentle bubbling. Sauce can be made ahead to this point; let cool and then cover and refrigerate for up to 2 days or freeze for up to 3 months.

Bolognese Sauce

½ cup (125 mL) olive oil

1 medium onion, diced

2½ lb (1.25 kg) ground veal

1 cup (250 mL) tomato paste (two 5.5 oz [156 mL] cans)

3 cups (750 mL) vegetable stock

2 large carrots, peeled and each one cut into 4 chunks

1 Tbsp (15 mL) sugar

½ tsp (2 mL) pepper

1 tsp (5 mL) salt

Serves 10.

Per serving: 786 cals, 34.4 g fat, 12.1 g sat. fat, 124 mg cholesterol, 798 mg sodium, 73.4 g carbs, 45.6 g protein

Beverage Suggestion: dry, medium-bodied red wine, such as Chianti; medium-dark beer

Pasta

While sauce is cooking, fill a very large pot with water and add salt; bring to a boil on high heat. Add pasta and stir; cook according to package directions until *al dente*. Stir frequently during cooking to prevent sticking. Drain pasta, rinse well with cold water, and drain again. Pasta can be made ahead to this point; let cool and store in a sealed plastic bag or covered container for up to 2 days.

Assembly and baking

Remove cooked pasta from the fridge 30 minutes before baking. Heat sauce on medium-low until warmed through, about 15 minutes; stir frequently to prevent sticking. Preheat the oven to 350°F (180°F) and oil a large, deep baking dish.

In a large bowl, mix pasta with warm sauce and pour into baking dish. Level out pasta and then evenly distribute cheese overtop, followed by parsley flakes.

Bake for 35 to 40 minutes, until pasta is heated through and cheese is melted. Preheat the broiler to high or 500°F (260°C). On second rack from top of oven, broil for 5 to 7 minutes until cheese is golden and crisp.

Pasta and Topping

2 Tbsp (30 mL) salt for pasta water
2 lb (1 kg) dried penne
vegetable oil for baking dish
4 cups (1 L) grated Edam cheese
2 Tbsp (30 mL) dried parsley flakes

Cooking Tips: Instead of vegetable stock, 3 cups (750 mL) hot water with 2 vegetable bouillon cubes may be used.

To make a richer sauce, add a 6 oz (175 g) piece of Parmesan cheese rind (ask at the deli) to the sauce for the full cooking period; remove before serving and discard.

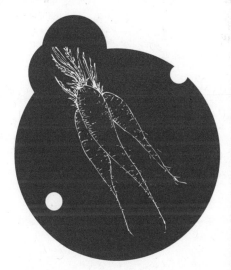

Linguine with Red Clam Sauce

One of my absolute favourites!

Place a large strainer with small holes in the sink. Bring a large pot of water with salt added to a boil. Add pasta and cook according to package directions, stirring frequently at first to separate pasta strands and then occasionally while cooking. It will take about 7 minutes of cooking for *al dente* and 8 to 9 minutes for tender.

While pasta is cooking, warm Marinara Sauce in a medium saucepan on medium-low, stirring occasionally. Add clams to sauce just before pasta is finished cooking and mix well. The clams are already cooked—you only want to reheat them gently, just before serving, so they don't become tough.

Drain pasta well and rinse with very hot water to remove salt. Portion out 4 servings of pasta; top each one with ¾ cup (185 mL) clam sauce and 1 tablespoon (15 mL) Parmesan, if using. Serve immediately and enjoy!

1 Tbsp (15 mL) salt for pasta water
1 lb (500 g) dried linguine
3 cups (750 mL) Marinara Sauce (p. 87)
two 7 oz (142 g) cans baby clams, drained and rinsed well
¼ cup (60 mL) Parmesan cheese for topping pasta (optional)

Serves 4.
Per serving (without Parmesan cheese):
573 cals, 4.2 g fat, 0.6 g sat. fat,
53 mg cholesterol, 1344 mg sodium,
103.4 g carbs, 30.4 g protein

Beverage Suggestion:
dry, medium-bodied red wine, such as
Merlot or Pinot Noir; pale ale or lager beer

Classic Spaghetti Carbonara

An excellent, easy, and quick choice when lack of time or hunger is a big issue!

Bring a large pot of water to a boil; add salt and spaghetti. Stir pasta with a pasta fork to get it all into the pot. Stir occasionally to separate the strands while it cooks. Cook according to package directions; spaghetti usually takes 8 to 9 minutes for *al dente* and 10 to 11 minutes for tender.

Separate 4 eggs and place yolks in a large bowl. (Whites can be frozen in a covered container for another use.) Add remaining 4 whole eggs to the yolks; whisk to combine. Mix in pepper and parsley. Set aside.

In a small saucepan, melt butter, add pancetta, and garlic, if using, and cook for 1 to 2 minutes on medium-low heat so it is hot and ready when you are ready to drain the pasta.

Drain pasta and rinse well with very hot water to wash off salt. Return to the warm pasta pot and add egg mixture, stirring constantly with a wooden spoon to combine. Add hot butter mixture and stir well. Mix in Parmesan and serve immediately.

Cooking Tips: This dish should be served immediately after mixing or it will cool down too much, so ready all your ingredients *before* adding them to the cooked pasta. If your dinner plates or a large (family-style) serving bowl are ovenproof, warming them beforehand will help maintain the temperature of the pasta. Just preheat the oven to the lowest setting, about 150°F (65°C), and place the dishes directly on the middle rack for 8 to 10 minutes. If desired, you can also add some cooked peas to this dish; add them to the hot butter mixture along with the garlic and pancetta.

Bringing eggs to room temperature: Place eggs in a bowl, fill it with hot water, and let stand for 5 minutes before draining off the water and discarding it.

1 lb (500 g) dried spaghetti or spaghettini

1 Tbsp (15 mL) salt for pasta water

8 large eggs, at room temperature, divided

½ tsp (2 mL) pepper

¼ cup (60 mL) freshly minced parsley, at room temperature (optional)

½ cup (125 mL) butter

4 oz (125 g) pancetta or 8 slices side bacon, chopped, cooked crisp, and drained well

1 tsp (5 mL) minced garlic (optional)

½ cup (125 mL) finely grated Parmesan cheese, at room temperature

Serves 4.

Per serving: 1018 cals, 57 g fat, 26.3 g sat. fat, 696 mg cholesterol, 771 mg sodium, 86.7 g carbs, 39.8 g protein

Beverage Suggestion:
dry, smooth white wine, such as Chardonnay

Stuffed Mac and Cheese

A new twist on an old classic! Purchase a 12 oz (375 g) block of cheddar cheese for this recipe.

Macaroni

1 Tbsp (15 mL) salt for the pasta water

1 lb (500 g) dried macaroni

Cheese Sauce

¼ cup (60 mL) butter

¼ cup (60 mL) flour

¼ cup (60 mL) white wine

1 cup (250 mL) whipping cream

1 tsp (5 mL) Dijon mustard

½ tsp (2 mL) garlic salt

½ tsp (2 mL) pepper

¼ tsp (1 mL) ground nutmeg

1 tsp (5 mL) Tabasco sauce or ½ tsp (2 mL) Chinese chili-garlic sauce

3 cups (750 mL) grated sharp cheddar cheese, divided

Serves 8.

Per serving: 872 cals, 53.3 g fat, 27.6 g sat. fat, 138 mg cholesterol, 1125 mg sodium, 64.9 g carbs, 32.8 g protein

Beverage Suggestion: dry, earthy white wine, such as Viognier; light beer

Macaroni

Heat a large pot of water to boiling and add salt. Add macaroni and stir well; boil until *al dente* (slightly chewy), stirring occasionally. Check pasta package for recommended cooking time.

Sauce

Melt butter in a medium-large saucepan on medium heat. Add flour and cook for 1 to 2 minutes, whisking the mixture to blend. Add wine and whisk until smooth. Pour in whipping cream and cook, stirring frequently, until sauces thickens, about 5 to 7 minutes. Add 2 cups (500 mL) water gradually, whisking frequently to prevent lumping. Cook for 10 to 15 minutes until sauce thickens again, stirring frequently with the whisk. Add the seasoning, mustard, and Tabasco or chili-garlic sauce, followed by 2 cups (500 mL) of the grated cheese. Mix well and cook until cheese is melted, about 2 to 3 minutes. Remove from heat.

Stuffing

In a covered medium skillet on medium-high heat, cook mushrooms and onions with butter and ¼ cup (60 mL) water for 5 minutes or until onions are transparent. Remove the lid and continue cooking for about 5 more minutes until water has evaporated and mushrooms and onions are light golden. Remove from heat. Add seasoning and bacon; mix well.

Assembly

In a medium bowl, mix breadcrumbs with olive oil and melted butter. Set aside.

Preheat the oven to 375°F (190°C) and oil a large, deep 4-quart (1 L) baking dish.

Drain pasta and rinse with hot water. Shake off excess water, then mix pasta into sauce. Pour half into the baking dish, levelling the add a spoon or knife. Evenly distribute mushroom stuffing overtop, add remaining pasta, and level the top again. Sprinkle evenly with remaining 1 cup (250 mL) grated cheese, followed by breadcrumb mixture and paprika and/or dried parsley, if using, for colour.

Bake pasta for 20 to 30 minutes to heat through, crisp the topping, and brown the edges.

Stuffing

8 oz (250 g) mushrooms, sliced ¼ inch (6 mm) thick

1 medium onion, diced

1 Tbsp (15 mL) butter

½ cup (125 mL) cooked, crumbled bacon (8 thin slices, diced, cooked crisp, drained well)

¼ tsp (1 mL) seasoning salt

¼ tsp (1 mL) pepper

Topping

1½ cups (375 mL) Panko breadcrumbs

1 Tbsp (15 mL) olive oil

1 Tbsp (15 mL) melted butter

½ tsp (2 mL) paprika and/or 1 Tbsp (15 mL) dried parsley flakes for garnishing (optional)

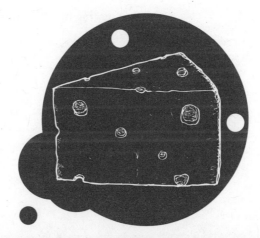

Chicken with Jalapeno and Lime

Sweet, tangy, and spicy—a great trio! Also try this marinade with fish or prawns.

½ cup (125 mL) orange juice concentrate, thawed

¼ cup (60 mL) honey

¼ cup (60 mL) lime juice

2 Tbsp (30 mL) seeded jalapeno peppers, finely chopped

1 Tbsp (15 mL) minced garlic

1 tsp (5 mL) lime zest

1 tsp (5 mL) ground cumin

¼ tsp (1 mL) salt

¼ tsp (1 mL) pepper

1½ lb (750 g) boneless and skinless chicken breasts or thighs

Serves 4.

Per serving: 378 cals, 2.3 g fat, 0.6 g sat. fat, 98 mg cholesterol, 260 mg sodium, 48.9 g carbs, 40.3 g protein

Beverage Suggestion: dry, fruity white wine such as Riesling or Gewürztraminer; lime margarita

In a medium-large bowl, whisk together all the ingredients except chicken. If using chicken breasts, slice each piece in half lengthwise to make 2 thinner pieces, about ½ to ¾ inch (1 to 2 cm) thick; if using thighs, cut each one into 3 rectangular pieces. Add chicken pieces to marinade and let stand, covered, in the fridge for at least 30 minutes but ideally for 1 to 2 hours.

Remove chicken from the fridge 30 minutes before grilling. Preheat the grill on medium-high and lightly oil it just before grilling. Remove chicken pieces from marinade, letting excess liquid drain off and back into the bowl. Place chicken pieces on the grill and cook until marked and golden around the edges, about 5 to 7 minutes. Brush chicken with some of the marinade in the first few minutes of cooking, then discard the remainder. With long, heatproof tongs, flip chicken pieces, and grill second side until also browned, about 5 minutes more. Transfer chicken from the grill to a warm serving dish; let stand, covered, for 5 minutes before serving.

Grilled Corn with Chili Lime Butter

There is nothing like fresh corn at a barbecue party. This recipe has a tangy twist for all those corn-on-the-cob lovers!

Preheat the grill on high. On the stove, bring a large pot of water with salt added to a boil. Boil corn for 7 to 8 minutes until tender.

In a small saucepan, melt butter with other ingredients on low heat to make Chili Lime Butter.

Dry off hot, cooked corn with a clean tea towel or paper towel, and then oil cobs lightly. Grill corn on high heat to create distinct grill marks, about 12 minutes per side. Place Chili Lime Butter in a medium bowl and roll each cob of corn in the butter to coat well, or drizzle 1 tablespoon (15 mL) over each cob. Serve immediately.

Cooking Tip: This recipe can be doubled or tripled easily. The butter can also be made ahead, covered, and refrigerated; melt it just before serving.

4 whole cobs of corn, shucked

2 tsp (10 mL) salt for the corn water

1 Tbsp (15 mL) vegetable oil or vegetable oil spray for the corn

Chili Lime Butter

¼ cup (60 mL) butter, roughly chopped

1 Tbsp (15 mL) lime juice

¼ tsp (1 mL) Worcestershire sauce

1 tsp (5 mL) chili powder

2¼ tsp (12 mL) salt

¼ tsp (2 mL) pepper

Serves 4.

Per cob with 1 Tbsp (15 mL) butter: 185 cals, 12.5 g fat, 7.3 g sat. fat, 31 mg cholesterol, 171 mg sodium, 15.4 g carbs, 2.7 g protein

Beverage Suggestion: Mexican beer; white sangria

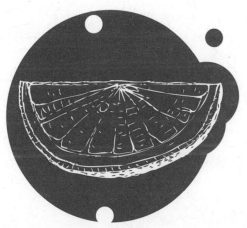

Texan Flank Steak

Flank steak is now a very trendy cut of meat! It is lean, tender, and delicious if you follow these basic principles: use a marinade or rub; cook it hot and fast; rest it long enough; and slice it thinly on a 45° angle. Start marinating the meat at least the day before so it has time to absorb all the great flavours.

¼ cup (60 mL) lime juice
2 Tbsp (30 mL) sugar
2 tsp (10 mL) salt
2 tsp (10 mL) pepper
1 tsp (5 mL) cayenne pepper
1 Tbsp (15 mL) chili powder
1½ tsp (7.5 mL) ground cumin
½ cup (125 mL) olive oil
1 tsp (5 mL) minced or puréed garlic
1 lb (500 g) beef flank steak
4 tsp (20 mL) butter for skillet if searing steak

Serves 4.

Per serving: 261 cals, 15.8 g fat, 4.6 g sat. fat, 56 mg cholesterol, 398 mg sodium, 6 g carbs, 23.6 g protein

Beverage Suggestion:
spicy, dry red wine, such as Syrah; red sangria; medium-dark beer

Marinating

In a small bowl, stir lime juice with sugar and salt until they dissolve. Add remaining ingredients, except for steak and butter; mix well. Add steak and marinade to a large Ziploc bag; remove any air and seal. Work marinade around in the bag to coat steak. (A glass, plastic, or stainless steel container can be used instead, provided steak can lay flat. Pour marinade overtop, turning meat to coat well, and then cover.) Marinate steak in the fridge for 8 hours, overnight, or up to 2 days.

Grilling

Before grilling or searing, allow 30 to 45 minutes for steak to return to room temperature after removing from the fridge. Preheat your grill on high to at least 400°F (200°C) for 15 minutes. Ready a covered dish or baking pan and foil for holding cooked steak.

Grill steak on high for 3 to 7 minutes per side depending on the thickness. (See facing page for exact grilling times.)

Alternately, sear steak on the stovetop in a 12-inch (30 cm) non-stick skillet on high heat with 2 teaspoons (10 mL) melted butter per side to help brown it; cook for the same amount of time as for grilling.

Rest steak, covered, in prepared dish for 10 to 15 minutes before slicing.

Slicing

Reserving any accumulated juice from the meat, place steak on a large cutting board with the longest side facing you. The "grain" of the meat should be visible and running lengthwise, from left to right; you are going to cut across this grain on a 45° angle. With a very sharp, long carving knife, cut thin slices about ¼ inch (6 mm) thick. Place slices on a serving platter and pour reserved meat juice overtop.

Cooking Tip: Steak that has marinated for 1 day can be wrapped well and frozen. Depending on the thickness of the steak, thawing will take at least 24 hours in the fridge; it is ready to cook once thawed.

Grilling times for flank steak: For a ½-inch (1 cm) steak, cook for 3 minutes per side; for a ¾-inch (2 cm) steak, cook for 4 to 5 minutes per side; and for 1-inch (2.5 cm) steak, cook for 7 minutes per side. These cooking times will render a rare steak after resting it; 1 to 2 minutes more per side will result in a medium-rare steak in the middle and well-done ends. Flank steak is best served rare for maximum tenderness and flavour.

Warm Potato Salad with Lemon Dijon Mayonnaise

This yummy dish is rich and creamy but remarkably light. The saltiness of the bacon goes well with the potatoes and it is a wonderful accompaniment to grilled meat or fish.

2 lb (1 kg) baby new potatoes, halved

2 Tbsp (30 mL) olive oil

7 oz (210 g) side bacon (6 regular slices), cooked crisp, drained, and diced

½ cup (125 mL) green onion (½ bunch), diced small

Lemon Dijon Dressing

⅔ cup (160 mL) mayonnaise

2 tsp (10 mL) grainy Dijon mustard

¼ tsp (1 mL) plain Dijon mustard

½ tsp (2 mL) lemon juice

¼ tsp (1 mL) pepper

¼ tsp (1 mL) onion salt

¼ tsp (1 mL) minced garlic

Serves 7.

Per serving: 335 cals, 23.5 g fat, 3.4 g sat. fat, 14 mg cholesterol, 421 mg sodium, 25.3 g carbs, 5.8 g protein

Beverage Suggestion: dry, smooth white wine, such as Chardonnay or Côtes-du-rhône

Preheat the oven to 400°F (200°C). In large, shallow baking pan, toss potatoes in olive oil until well coated. Bake potatoes, cut side up, in the bottom third of the oven for 15 minutes; flip and bake for another 10 to 20 minutes, until tender in the middle and light golden in colour. Very small potatoes (1½ inches [4 cm] across) will take 10 minutes to finish while small ones (2 to 2½ inches [5 to 6 cm]) across will take 15 to 20 minutes to finish. In the last 5 minutes of cooking potatoes, sprinkle them with bacon bits.

While potatoes are cooking (or earlier in the day, or even the day before), prepare bacon, green onions, and dressing.

To make Lemon Dijon Dressing, mix mayonnaise with other ingredients in a small bowl, and stir until well combined. Cover and refrigerate until 20 minutes before assembling the salad; dressing should be at room temperature for serving.

Ready a medium-large bowl and wooden spoon for tossing potatoes with dressing. Remove potato/bacon mixture from the oven and add to the bowl. Add dressing and mix well with the wooden spoon. Spoon salad onto a serving platter, or into a serving bowl, and top with green onions. Serve immediately.

Cooking Tip: Chopped chives can be substituted for the green onions if desired.

Halibut au Gratin

Here's a way to get any kids, big or small, to eat fish! Try any type of white fish that fits your budget. A small food processor makes preparing the breadcrumb topping a snap.

Preheat the oven to 350°F (180°C) and oil a large baking pan or baking sheet.

Melt butter in a small saucepan on low heat; mix in olive oil. Brush or drizzle onto fish portions, coating both sides. Add fish to prepared baking pan and bake for 10 minutes in the bottom third of the oven. While fish is cooking, mix topping ingredients together.

Remove fish from the oven. Turn the temperature to broil or 500°F (260°C).

Top each piece of fish with about ⅓ cup (80 mL) of the topping, pressing down lightly to adhere it. Broil fish on second rack from top of oven for 3 to 4 minutes until golden brown. Remove from the oven and serve immediately.

four 6 oz (175 g) skinless halibut fillets, ¾ inch thick (or 1½ lb [750 g] halibut if filleting at home)

2 Tbsp (30 mL) butter

1 Tbsp (15 mL) olive oil

Topping

⅔ cup (160 mL) fresh breadcrumbs

¼ tsp (1 mL) pepper

¼ tsp (1 mL) salt

⅛ tsp (0.5 mL) onion powder

⅔ cup (160 mL) grated sharp or aged cheddar cheese

1 tsp (5 mL) dried parsley flakes

Serves 4.

Per serving: 439 cals, 22.5 g fat, 9.9 g sat. fat, 110 mg cholesterol, 499 mg sodium, 13.7 g carbs, 45.4 g protein

Beverage Suggestion:
Buttery, dry white wine, such as Chardonnay; light, refreshing fruit-based cocktail

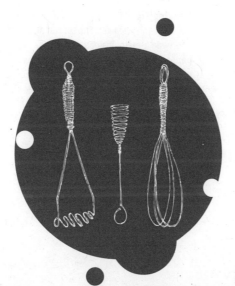

Zucchini Lace Fritters

Crispy, light, and delicious! Make larger ones for a vegetable side dish, or little ones for appetizers. Try them drizzled with Lemon Feta Dip (p. 131).

4 cups (1 L) coarsely grated zucchini (2 medium-large)

¼ cup (60 mL) green onion, finely chopped (3 medium)

¼ cup (60 mL) rice flour

1 tsp (5 mL) fresh dill or mint, finely minced

½ tsp (2 mL) pepper

½ tsp (2 mL) salt

1 large egg white, lightly beaten

1 cup (250 mL) canola oil or corn oil for frying

sour cream for serving (optional)

Makes 12 fritters.

Per fritter (without condiments): 54 cals, 2.6 g fat, 0.3 g sat. fat, 105 mg sodium, 5.2 g carbs, 2.5 g protein

Beverage Suggestion: dry apple or pear cider

Preheat the oven to 250°F (120°C) and line a baking sheet with paper towels. In a large bowl, combine zucchini and green onion. Add rice flour and seasonings; mix well. Stir in egg white to coat well.

In a large non-stick skillet, heat cooking oil, 1 inch (2.5 cm) deep, on medium-high until rippling. With a spoon, place ⅓ cup (80 mL) portions of batter into the oil, spaced 3 to 4 inches (8 to 10 cm) apart; flatten the tops with the spoon to make them ¼ inch (6 mm) thick and about 3½ to 4 inches (9 to 10 cm) across. Cook fritters for 1 to 2 minutes, until the underside is golden; flip and brown the other side for 1 to 2 minutes more. Drain fritters on paper towels and keep warm in the oven. Repeat process until all the batter is used up.

Serve fritters warm with sour cream on the side, if desired.

Cooking Tips: All-purpose white flour can be substituted for rice flour but the "lace" will be slightly heavier. Fritters can also be made with potato, or a combination of potato and sweet potato, instead of zucchini. Try adding spices, such as curry or cayenne pepper, for a change but omit the herbs if you do. Appetizer-size fritters can be made using 1 to 1½ tablespoon (15 to 22.5 mL) batter per fritter. They will take less time to cook than the larger ones; 1 minute per side or until golden brown.

Candied Beef Tenderloin with Balsamic Butter

The sweet and salty coating goes great with the balsamic vinegar and black pepper!

Steaks

Mix salt, sugar, and pepper together in a medium bowl. Dip each steak in the mixture, coating all sides, about 1 tablespoon (15 mL) per steak. Set aside on a plate for 30 minutes to bring to room temperature before grilling.

Lightly oil the grill and preheat on medium-high or to 400°F (200°C). Sear steaks for 5 to 7 minutes per side to brown and cook to your liking. (See below for exact grilling times.) Transfer steaks to a plate after cooking, cover with foil or another plate, and let stand while you make the Balsamic Butter.

Balsamic Butter

In a medium skillet, heat vinegar to boiling on medium-high and add shallots. Cook until shallots are transparent and vinegar has reduced to 2 tablespoons (30 mL), about 5 to 7 minutes. Remove from heat and gradually whisk in butter.

Serve steaks drizzled with 1½ to 2 tablespoons (22.5 to 30 mL) sauce each.

Grilling times for tenderloin steaks: Grill steaks on an oiled grill preheated on medium-high. For medium-rare, grill 1-inch (2.5 cm) thick steaks for 5 minutes per side, 7 minutes per side if 1½ inches (4 cm) thick, or 8 minutes per side if 2 inches (5 cm) thick. Remove steaks from the grill, cover, and let stand for 5 to 8 minutes before serving. Remember that they will continue to cook so they should be slightly undercooked when removed from the grill.

Steaks

2 Tbsp (30 mL) grated sea salt, coarsely ground salt, or fleur de sel

2 Tbsp (30 mL) raw sugar

1 Tbsp (15 mL) coarsely cracked pepper

four 7 to 8 oz (200 to 250 g) beef tenderloin steaks, 1½ to 2 inches (4 to 5 cm) thick

Balsamic Butter

¼ cup (60 mL) balsamic vinegar

2 Tbsp (30 mL) minced shallots

¼ cup (60 mL) cold butter, diced

Serves 4.

Per 8 oz (250 g) steak with 2 Tbsp (30 mL) sauce: 503 cals, 32.7 g fat, 15.3 g sat. fat, 175 mg cholesterol, 910 mg sodium, 4.7 g carbs, 47.4 g protein

Beverage Suggestion: smooth, dry red wine, such as Côtes-du-rhône or Beaujolais

Mocha Chili Rubbed Steaks

Rich but mellow at the same time with a hint of heat that you will love!

1 recipe Mocha Chili Rub (p. 103)

four 8-oz (250 g) New York striploin steaks, preferably cut 1½ inch (4 cm) thick

vegetable oil for the grill

Serves 4.

Per steak: 415 cals, 20.2 g fat, 7.1 g sat. fat, 117 mg cholesterol, 745 mg sodium, 5.1 g carbs, 53.4 g protein

Beverage Suggestion: dry, spicy red wine, such as Syrah

Place rub in a medium bowl. Dip each steak in the mixture and thinly coat with about 2 teaspoons (10 mL). Set steaks aside on a plate for 30 minutes to bring to room temperature before grilling.

Lightly oil the grill and preheat to 400°F (200°C). Grill steaks to your liking, about 4 to 5 minutes per side for medium-rare if 1½ inches (4 cm) thick. Let steaks rest on a plate, covered, for 5 minutes before serving so they are juicier. Remember that they will continue cooking so they should be slightly undercooked when removed from the grill.

Shopping Tip: For the best flavour, choose beef aged at least 21 to 28 days. The colour of the beef should be dark red. Bright red or pink-coloured meat is from beef that has only been aged about 2 weeks—it will definitely not be as tasty.

Mocha Chili Rub

One batch of Mocha Chili Rub will coat four New York striploin or rib-eye steaks, or up to six beef tenderloins; pick your favourite grilling steak for this recipe.

In a small bowl, whisk together seasonings, crushing any lumps with the back of a spoon and mixing them in. Store in an airtight container for up to 1 month.

1 Tbsp (15 mL) brown sugar

2 tsp (10 mL) chili powder

2 tsp (10 mL) instant coffee powder

1 tsp (5 mL) dark Dutch cocoa powder, sifted to remove lumps

1 tsp (5 mL) salt

1 tsp (5 mL) pepper

½ tsp (2 mL) cinnamon

⅛ tsp (0.5 mL) cayenne pepper

Makes 3½ tablespoons (52.5 mL).

Per 3.5 Tbsp (52.5 mL): 97 cals, 1.1 g fat, 0.2 g sat. fat, 2415 mg sodium, 20.2 g carbs. 1.4 g protein

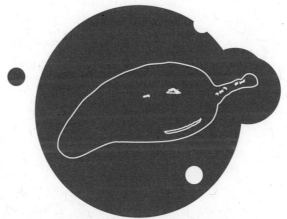

Hot Potatoes

A spicy version of baked stuffed potatoes with a Mexican flair!

6 large russet potatoes, about 9 or 10 oz [270 to 300 g] each, unpeeled, scrubbed and dried

2 Tbsp (30 mL) butter, at room temperature

¼ cup (60 mL) sour cream

¼ tsp (1 mL) garlic salt

¼ tsp (1 mL) salt

¼ tsp (1 mL) pepper

¼ tsp (1 mL) Tabasco sauce

1 cup (250 mL) grated Monterey Jack or Edam cheese, divided

¼ cup (60 mL) canned chopped mild green chilies, rinsed and drained

2 Tbsp (30 mL) cilantro leaves, finely chopped

1 cup (250 mL) Fresh Salsa (p. 127) or purchased deli-style salsa (optional)

additional sour cream (optional)

Serves·6.

Per serving (without salsa or sour cream):
246 cals, 8.2 g fat, 4.3 g sat. fat,
17 mg cholesterol, 412 mg sodium,
34.1 g carbs, 8.9 g protein

Beverage Suggestion:
Mexican beer, such as Corona or Dos Equis

Preheat the oven to 400°F (200°C). Poke several holes in each potato with a skewer or fork; place in a baking pan. Bake for 1 hour and 15 minutes, or until tender throughout when poked with a skewer. Cool potatoes for 20 to 30 minutes, until they are cool enough to handle.

Make a lengthwise slice to remove top third of each potato. Scoop out cooked potato from the "lids" and insides, leaving shells ⅓ to ½ inch (8 mm to 1 cm) thick. Place cooked potato in a medium bowl with butter and set aside. Discard lids.

In a small bowl, mix together sour cream and seasonings. Add to the buttery potato and mash thoroughly with a potato masher. Stir vigorously with the masher in a circular motion for 1 to 2 minutes to help smooth mixture and remove any lumps. Stir in ⅔ cup (160 mL) of the cheese, along with chilies and cilantro.

Divide seasoned potato filling evenly between potato shells and top with remaining cheese, about 1 tablespoon (15 mL) per potato. You can prepare potatoes ahead to this point; cover and refrigerate for up to 1 day. Remove from the fridge at least 30 minutes prior to baking.

Preheat the oven to 400°F (200°C) and oil a large baking dish. Bake potatoes, spaced at least 1 to 2 inches (2.5 to 5 cm) apart, for 25 minutes, or until golden on top and heated through. Serve with salsa and sour cream on the side, if desired.

Potato Chip Gratin

If you like crispy potatoes, you are going to love this dish! A Japanese vegetable slicer (or mandoline) and a pastry brush make this recipe easy and quick. Purchase finely grated Parmesan from the deli so the cheese sticks nicely to the butter on the potatoes; shredded cheese is too coarse for this job!

Preheat the oven to 450°F (240°C). Grease an 8 × 12 inch (20 × 30 cm) or 10 × 10 inch (25 × 25 cm) baking pan with about 2 teaspoons (10 mL) of the melted butter.

Lay potato slices in the pan in long rows, overlapping each other like dominos and staggered by about ¼ inch (6 mm). The rows should look like a deck of cards that a dealer has fanned out with one hand. Create as many rows as the dish will accommodate, ideally 4 or 5 rows.

Brush potatoes with remaining butter, thoroughly coating the top, and then lightly sprinkle with salt and more liberally with pepper. Finish by sprinkling Parmesan cheese overtop. Bake for 20 to 25 minutes in the bottom third of the oven until golden brown and potatoes are very crispy.

3 Tbsp (45 mL) melted butter, divided

1 lb (500 g) red potatoes (about 4 medium), sliced ⅛ inch (3 mm) thick, unpeeled

¼ tsp (1 mL) pepper in a shaker

⅛ tsp (0.5 mL) salt in a shaker

⅓ cup (80 mL) Parmesan cheese, finely grated

Serves 4.

Per serving: 215 cals, 11.2 g fat, 7 g sat. fat, 30 mg cholesterol, 237 mg sodium, 22.1 g carbs, 6.1 g protein

Beverage Suggestion:
Chardonnay

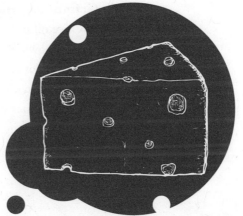

Tempura Fish with Lemon Caper Sauce

Light, crisp batter; tender, moist fish; and creamy, tangy sauce. Pair with Double Fried French Fries (p. 58) and you have fish and chips perfection!

eight 3 oz (90 g) pieces Pacific Grey cod or halibut, ½ inch (1 cm) thick (about 1½ lb [750 g])

salt and pepper in shakers or grinders

1 to 1½ cups (375 to 500 mL) canola oil for deep-frying

¾ cup (185 mL) flour

12 oz (355 mL) can club soda

1 recipe Lemon Caper Sauce (p. 107)

Makes 8 pieces of battered fish.
Per piece with 2 Tbsp (60 mL) sauce: 329 cals, 25.2 g fat, 2.6 g sat. fat, 40 mg cholesterol, 472 mg sodium, 8.9 g carbs, 16.6 g protein

Beverage Suggestion:
crisp, dry white wine, such as Sauvignon Blanc; pale ale beer

Line a baking dish with paper towels to drain fish after frying. Pat fish portions dry with paper towels, then salt and pepper all sides.

Fill a large, deep skillet at least 1 inch (2.5 cm) deep with oil but do not exceed one-quarter of the pan's total depth. Oil level will rise when the fish is added so you do not want to overfill the pan. If using a deep fryer, preheat oil according to manufacturer's directions to about 375°F (190°C), or heat oil in the skillet on medium-high until rippling but not smoking. Mix the batter while oil preheats.

In a medium bowl, whisk flour with ¾ cup (185 mL) club soda. Batter will be lumpy at first but will smooth out after 30 to 60 seconds of continued whisking. If still very thick and sticky, add 2 tablespoons (30 mL) additional soda and whisk to smooth, repeating if necessary. Batter should be thick but pourable like cake batter. You want it to coat the fish when you dip pieces in the bowl; if it isn't runny enough, add more soda.

Once oil is hot, coat fish with batter, letting any excess fall back into the bowl. Place fish into the hot oil carefully using heatproof tongs. Do not crowd the pieces; cook them in at least 2 batches. Fry for about 3 to 4 minutes per side until light golden brown; flip and brown the other side. Fish and batter coating should feel firm when pressed with tongs. Repeat procedure to cook remaining fish. Serve immediately with Lemon Caper Sauce on the side.

Lemon Caper Sauce

An easy and delicious sauce for fish; it falls somewhere between tartar sauce and aïoli. Use any leftover sauce to make fantastic tuna salad sandwiches.

In a small bowl, mix together all the ingredients until well incorporated. Cover and refrigerate for up to 1 week. The sauce should sit for several hours in the fridge before serving to help the flavours blend.

½ cup (125 mL) whole-egg mayonnaise such as Hellman's or Kraft Real Mayo

1 tsp (5 mL) lemon juice

1 Tsp (5 mL) olive oil

¼ tsp (1 mL) salt

⅛ tsp (0.5 mL) pepper

⅛ tsp (0.5 mL) onion powder

¼ tsp (1 mL) finely minced or puréed garlic

1 Tbsp (15 mL) capers, chopped fine

1 Tbsp (15 mL) fresh parsley leaves, finely minced

Makes ⅔ cup (160 mL).

Per Tbsp (15 mL): 69 cals, 7.7 g fat, 0.8 g sat. fat, 4 mg cholesterol, 146 mg sodium, 0.1 g protein

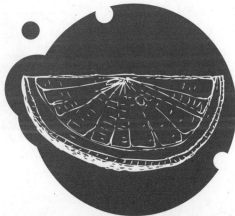

Fish and Chips

Whenever I buy fish and chips, the fish is hot but the fries are cold. Here's a way to have them both hot and fresh!

1 recipe Tempura Fish with
Lemon Caper Sauce (p. 106)
1 recipe Double Fried French Fries (p. 58)
ketchup for dipping chips (optional)
malt vinegar for sprinkling
on the chips (optional)

Serves 4.

Per 1 piece fish, 8 oz (250 g) chips, and 2 Tbsp
(30 mL) sauce (without additional condiments):
788 cals, 54.5 g fat, 5.3 g sat. fat,
48 mg cholesterol, 778 mg sodium,
52.4 g carbs, 21.8 g protein

Beverage Suggestion:
crisp, dry white wine, such as
Sauvignon Blanc; pale ale beer

Prepare the Lemon Caper Sauce; set aside.

Do the first fry of the French fries while you prep the fish batter. Fill a deep fryer and/or deep non-stick skillet(s) with recommended amount of oil. Follow recipes for cooking fish and fries but keep in mind that cooking times need to be coordinated as follows.

Preheat the oil for the fish first since cooking time is 3 to 4 minutes per side, or 6 to 8 minutes in total. Fries will only take about 2 to 3 minutes total to brown so only preheat the oil for cooking them just before starting to fry the fish.

Start the second fry of the French fries just after you flip the fish to cook the second side.

Serve immediately, after draining, while both fish and fries are hot and crispy.

Prime Rib Roast with Red Wine Gravy

The perfect choice for a special occasion and easy to make for a crowd. Yields a medium-rare roast inside with medium to well-done slices at each end. The cooking time and method will work for any size of standing rib, even a whole one with 10 to 11 ribs. A four-rib roast will feed up to six people, or four people with enough leftovers to make Balsamic Beef Paninis (p. 27). Start the roast by 3:00 PM for a 7:00 PM dinner.

Preheat the oven to 375°F (190°C) and lightly oil a large baking dish or roaster. Pat roast dry with paper towels and add it to the prepared pan.

In a small bowl, mix mustard and seasonings together with a spoon, and then spread over top and sides of roast. Pour wine into the bottom of the pan.

Roast beef for 1 hour, and then turn the oven off. Keep roast in the oven with the door shut.

One hour before dinner, turn the oven to 300°F (150°C) and finish roast by cooking for 45 minutes. Remove and let stand, covered, for 15 minutes before carving.

Slice roast across the grain or parallel to the ribs. You can cut the ribs off and serve them on the side: slice down between them and the inner rib-eye roast all along the length of the roast. Slice roast, across the grain, to desired thickness. Serve sliced roast beef with Wine Gravy on the side.

5 lb (2.2 kg) standing rib (prime rib) roast with ribs attached, at room temperature

2 Tbsp (30 mL) Dijon mustard

2 tsp (10 mL) finely chopped fresh rosemary (do not substitute dried)

½ tsp (2 mL) coarse sea salt

½ tsp (2 mL) coarsely ground pepper

½ cup (125 mL) dry red wine

vegetable oil for baking dish or roaster

1 recipe Wine Gravy (p. 110) prepared using roast drippings and beef stock

Serves 6.

Per serving with ⅓ cup (80 mL) gravy: 621 cals, 32 g fat, 12.2 g sat. fat, 227 mg cholesterol, 690 mg sodium, 6.2 g carbs, 77.2 g protein

Beverage Suggestion:
robust, dry red wine, such as Cabernet Sauvignon or Bordeaux

Portioning Prime Rib: It is traditional to cut prime rib slices quite thick, about ½ to ¾ inch (1 to 2 cm), and serve 6 to 8 oz (175 to 250 g) portions, which is a substantial amount. If you cut the roast into thinner slices, about ⅛ to ¼ inch (3 to 4 mm), it is easier to adjust the portion size—and the meat seems to go further this way when you have a big group.

Wine Gravy

I devised this recipe for gravy lovers who don't want to cook a roast or chicken to get great gravy, and the big bonus is that it is fat-free!

¼ cup (60 mL) dry white or red wine (use white with chicken stock and red with beef stock)

4 cups (1 L) low-sodium chicken or beef stock, divided

½ tsp (2 mL) paprika, sifted to remove lumps

½ tsp (2 mL) pepper

½ tsp (2 mL) salt

⅛ tsp (0.5 mL) onion powder

⅛ tsp (0.5 mL) garlic granules or garlic powder

½ to 1 tsp (2 to 5 mL) sugar

½ cup (125 mL) flour

Makes 3 cups (750 mL).

Per ⅓ cup (80 mL): 28 cals, 298 mg sodium, 6.1 g carbs, 0.7 g protein

In a medium-large saucepan, bring wine and 3 cups (750 mL) of the stock to a boil on medium-high heat. To concentrate the flavour, cook for about 10 minutes until liquid is reduced to 2 cups (500 mL).

Reduce the heat to medium-low. Add the seasoning and ½ teaspoon (2 mL) sugar; mix well.

In a medium bowl, whisk flour with remaining 1 cup (250 mL) stock. Stock-wine reduction should be hot but not boiling when adding the flour mixture; if necessary, remove pot from heat, and wait until it stops. Strain flour mixture through a sieve into the simmering pot and whisk immediately until smooth.

Cook on medium-low heat for 3 to 4 minutes, stirring frequently with a whisk to prevent lumps from forming as gravy thickens. Turn the heat down to the lowest setting and simmer until needed (for up to 30 minutes); cover to prevent a skin from forming. If gravy gets too thick, you can whisk in ¼ cup (60 mL) water to dilute it. Before serving, taste gravy to see if it needs the additional ½ teaspoon (2 mL) of sugar and whisk in if desired.

Cooking Tips: As you would do with tomato sauce because of its acidity, adding sugar to the gravy smoothes out the tanginess of the wine. It is not always needed; it depends on the wine used.

If you cook a roast or chicken, you can still use this recipe but add the wine to the pan used to cook the meat. You can also add some of the stock to the pan to keep the meat moist and use it for basting. When the meat is cooked, strain off the juices, separating and discarding the fat, and then add to the gravy for extra flavour.

Showtime Snacks & Party Pleasers

112 Peppered Pecans

113 Curried Cashews

114 Red Hot Peanuts

115 Bar Brittle

116 Salt and Pepper Sesame Snacks

117 Nuts and Bolts

118 Parmesan Veggie Chips

120 Party Pretzels

121 Homemade Potato Chips

122 Seasoned Popcorn

124 Black Bean Dip with Chips

125 Chili Con Queso Dip
     with Tortilla Chips

126 Tex-Mex Tortilla Chips
     with Fresh Salsa

127 Mexican Seasoning

127 Fresh Salsa

128 Salami Chips with
     Cream Cheese Dip

129 Cream Cheese Dip

130 Wonton Crisps with
     Sweet and Sour Dipping Sauce

131 Fresh Vegetables with
     Lemon Feta Dip

Peppered Pecans

Pepper goes great with nuts; most people think of salt first, but both are equally tasty and the pepper kicks it up a notch.

2 cups (500 mL) raw pecan halves (about ½ lb [250 g])

1 Tbsp (15 mL) melted butter

2 tsp (10 mL) Worcestershire sauce

¼ tsp (1 mL) Tabasco sauce (about 3 dashes)

¼ tsp (1 mL) salt

½ tsp (2 mL) freshly ground pepper, divided

Makes 2 cups (500 mL).

Per ¼ cup (60 mL): 226 cals, 21.5 g fat, 2.5 g sat. fat, 4 mg cholesterol, 90 mg sodium, 5.8 g carbs, 2.3 g protein

Beverage Suggestion: dry, spicy red wine, such as Syrah

Preheat the oven to 300°F (150°C).

In a medium bowl, toss nuts with melted butter, sauces, and seasonings. Spread nuts out on an ungreased baking sheet in a single layer. Bake for 20 minutes, stirring nuts after 10 minutes.

Cool for 20 minutes so nuts crisp up before serving. Grind a bit of additional pepper on top of nuts as they cool. Cool completely; store in an airtight container for up to 2 weeks.

Curried Cashews

These nuts will cure your craving for cashews—and that curry craving! Use my recipe for Garam Masala (see Cooking Tip) or purchase it from the spice section of the grocery store.

Preheat the oven to 250°F (120°C).

In a medium bowl, toss cashews with melted butter and seasoning. Spread nuts in a single layer on an ungreased baking sheet. Bake in the middle of the oven for 20 minutes, stirring after 10 minutes.

Cool for 20 minutes so nuts crisp up before serving. Store in an airtight container for up to 2 weeks.

Cooking Tip: To make your own Garam Masala, mix together 1 tablespoon (15 mL) of each of the following ground spices: ginger (sift first), cardamon, cumin, coriander, curry, and cinnamon. Store in an airtight container for up to 3 months. Makes 6 tablespoons (90 mL).

2 cups (500 mL) unsalted roasted cashews (about ½ lb [250 g])
1 Tbsp (5 mL) melted butter
1 Tbsp (15 mL) Garam Masala seasoning
½ tsp (2 mL) salt

Makes 2 cups (500 mL).
Per ¼ cup (60 mL): 214 cals, 16.2 g fat, 3.2 g sat. fat, 1 mg cholesterol, 5 mg sodium, 11.7 g carbs, 5.3 g protein

Beverage Suggestion:
dry, fruity white wine, such as Riesling or Gewürztraminer

Red Hot Peanuts

These nuts will kick-start the party!

2 cups (500 mL) unsalted roasted peanuts
1 Tbsp (15 mL) olive oil
1 Tbsp (15 mL) lime juice
1½ tsp (7 mL) paprika
1 tsp (5 mL) salt
½ tsp (2 mL) cayenne pepper

Makes 2 cups (500 mL).
Per ¼ cup (60 mL): 232 cals, 18.2 g fat,
2.5 g sat. fat, 298 mg sodium,
8.4 g carbs, 8.7 g protein

Beverage Suggestion:
ice cold Mexican or light beer

Preheat the oven to 250°F (120°C).

In a medium bowl, toss peanuts with oil and seasonings. Spread nuts out on an ungreased baking sheet in a single layer. Bake nuts in the middle of the oven for 20 minutes, stirring after 10 minutes.

Cool for 20 minutes so nuts firm up before serving. Store in an airtight container for up to 2 weeks.

Cooking Tip: If you are substituting raw peanuts, bake them first at 300°F (150°C) for 20 minutes, stirring after 10 minutes.

Bar Brittle

I love these salty and sweet combinations—they're a big hit at holiday time. Try using Red Hot Peanuts (p. 114) for Red Hot Brittle.

Cover a baking sheet with aluminum foil and oil lightly with vegetable oil; set aside on a cooling rack.

In a large non-stick skillet, melt butter with corn syrup on medium-high heat. Add sugar and mix with a wooden spoon just enough to moisten. Cook, without stirring, for 4 to 5 minutes until the middle starts to caramelize—you will see it turning from yellow to light brown. Stir to incorporate caramel into rest of mixture. With a dinner knife or spoon, remove any sugar stuck to the wooden spoon and return it to the skillet to cook.

After 2 to 3 minutes, when mixture is light to medium gold in colour, add nuts and stir to incorporate. Continue cooking for 1 to 2 minutes more to completely caramelize mixture, until golden brown in colour. Do not touch; mixture is extremely hot and can easily burn your skin.

Spread liquid brittle on prepared baking sheet, trying to form a single layer of nuts if possible. While brittle is still hot, sprinkle surface with salt (and possibly pepper; see Cooking Tip). Let fully cool and harden before touching, at least 30 minutes.

Break into 1½-inch (4 cm) square pieces. Store brittle in a covered, foil-lined tin for 7 to 10 days. You can also store it in an airtight container but brittle will soften after about 5 days in a humid climate.

aluminum foil for baking sheet

1 to 2 tsp (5 to 10 mL) vegetable oil or non-stick spray oil for baking sheet

¼ cup (60 mL) butter

¼ cup (60 mL) white corn syrup

1⅓ cups (330 mL) sugar

3 cups (750 mL) flavoured peanuts, such as Salt & Pepper, Chili Lime, or Barbecue

⅛ tsp (0.5 mL) salt or seasoning salt (see Cooking Tip)

Makes about 6 cups (1.5 L).

Per ¼ cup (60 mL): 143 cals, 11 g fat, 2.4 g sat. fat, 5 mg cholesterol, 165 mg sodium, 6.8 g carbs, 4.3 g protein

Beverage Suggestion:
pale ale or lager beer

Cooking Tip: I sprinkle sea salt and freshly ground pepper on the Salt & Pepper brittle and use seasoning salt for Chili Lime, Barbecue, and Red Hot brittles.

Salt and Pepper Sesame Snacks

Since sesame seeds combine so well with sweet and salty ingredients, why not use both? This recipe gives you the chance to choose whether you want to use a trans-fat-free, cholesterol-free margarine or use butter, which has no trans-fats but which does have cholesterol.

parchment paper or vegetable oil for pan

3 Tbsp (45 mL) spreadable margarine or 2 Tbsp (30 mL) butter plus 1 Tbsp (15 mL) water

3 Tbsp (45 mL) packed brown sugar

2 Tbsp (30 mL) honey

1 Tbsp (15 mL) water

½ tsp (2 mL) salt

¼ tsp (1 mL) vanilla

¾ cup (185 mL) toasted sesame seeds

2 cups (500 mL) roasted salted peanuts

¼ tsp (1 mL) pepper (optional)

Makes 10 bars.

Per bar (made with butter): 288 cals, 21.1 g fat, 4 g sat. fat, 249 mg sodium, 15.4 g carbs, 9.2 g protein

Beverage Suggestion:
honey lager or medium-dark beer

Preheat the oven to 350°F (180°C) and line an 8-inch (20 cm) square baking pan with parchment paper, or oil it liberally.

In a medium saucepan, on medium heat, melt margarine or butter with sugar, honey, water, salt, and vanilla; cook for 3 to 5 minutes, just until sugar is melted and mixture is smooth. Remove from heat and add seeds and peanuts; mix well. Spread mixture into prepared pan and level the top with a spatula. Sprinkle with pepper, if desired.

Bake for 8 minutes; turn the baking pan around for even browning and bake another 7 minutes. Cool for at least 5 minutes but not more than 10 minutes or mixture will harden completely.

Using a sharp knife, deeply score or cut through the mixture to make 2 equal pieces. Score or cut each half into 5 equal bars, about 4 × 1.6 inches (4 × 10 cm). Cool bars completely before removing from pan. If you scored them instead of cutting them, bars should snap apart for you.

Nuts and Bolts

A family favourite at Christmas because that was the only time of the year my mother ever made it—her recipe actually made *double* this amount. You will need an extra-large turkey roaster to bake it in, or divide up the mixture and bake it in batches. It makes an excellent hostess gift for casual gatherings.

Preheat the oven to 250°F (120°C). In a medium bowl or large measuring cup, whisk together oil, Worcestershire sauce, and seasonings. Mix dry cereals, pretzels, and nuts together in 2 or 3 extra-large bowls. Repeatedly drizzle small amounts of seasoned oil overtop, mixing well with a spatula after each addition.

Bake Nuts and Bolts in a large roaster, in batches if necessary, for 90 minutes, stirring every 20 to 25 minutes.

Cool completely and store in airtight containers or Ziploc freezer bags for up to 2 weeks in a humid climate or up to 4 weeks in a dry climate.

1 cup (250 mL) canola or corn oil

1 Tbsp (15 mL) Worcestershire sauce

½ tsp (2 mL) garlic powder

½ tsp (2 mL) seasoning salt

2 tsp (10 mL) salt

medium (525 g) box regular Cheerios

small box (350 to 400 g) regular Crispix or Shreddies

8 oz (250 g) bag low-sodium pretzel sticks, such as Safeway Eating Right brand

10 oz (300 g) can mixed nuts

Makes 37 cups (9.25 L).

Per 1 cup (250 mL): 222 cals, 11.6 g fat, 1.2 g sat. fat, 551 mg sodium, 25.5 g carbs, 4 g protein

Beverage Suggestion:
Caesar or Bloody Mary; medium-bodied beer; cola

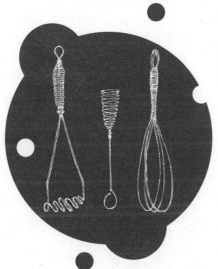

Parmesan Veggie Chips

A handheld Japanese slicer (or a mandoline) makes for thin and even vegetable slices. The vegetables are prepared and cooked separately because each cooking time varies, and the beets will stain the other vegetables if combined prior to frying.

1 large russet potato (about 12 oz [375 g]), peeled

2 large parsnips (about 12 oz [375 g]), peeled

3 medium whole beets (about 12 oz [375 g]), greens trimmed to 1 inch (2.5 cm), skins left on

3 cups (750 mL) canola oil for deep-frying, or correct amount for your deep fryer

¼ cup (60 mL) grated Parmesan cheese

½ tsp (2 mL) freshly ground pepper

Makes about 12 cups (3 L), which serves 8 as a snack or appetizer.

Per 1½ cup (375 mL): 196 cals, 11.4 g fat, 1.3 g sat. fat, 2 mg cholesterol, 98 mg sodium, 20.1 g carbs, 3.4 g protein

Beverage Suggestion: dry apple or pear cider

Beet preparation

Bring to a boil a medium-large pot of water and add beets. Gently boil until tender inside when poked with a fork or skewer, about 20 minutes depending on size. Drain and cool before rubbing off skins and any root ends; set aside. Beets can be cooked the day before; cover and refrigerate until 30 minutes before deep-frying.

Just before frying, set slicer to thinnest setting, about ¹⁄₃₂ inch (1 mm). Wearing gloves if your hands stain from beet juice, slice beets straight across for round chips, or on an angle for larger, oblong chips. Blot dry on paper towels; set aside.

Potato preparation

Fill a large bowl with cold water for soaking slices. Set slicer to thinnest setting, about ¹⁄₃₂ inch (1 mm), and slice potatoes straight across for round chips, or on an angle for larger, oblong chips. Soak slices in water for at least 20 minutes. Rinse off starchy water, drain slices well, and lay between two clean tea towels to dry.

Parsnip preparation

Fill a medium-large bowl with cold water. Set slicer to thinnest setting, about ¹⁄₃₂ inch (1 mm), and slice peeled parsnips on an angle. Place slices in cold water to prevent browning and soak for 20 minutes. Drain and dry them the same way as for the potatoes.

Cooking the chips

Line a baking pan with paper towels for draining hot chips. Fill a large 4 to 5 inch (10 to 12 cm) deep pan with 1 inch (2.5 cm) oil and preheat on medium-high until oil is rippling but not smoking, or preheat a pre-filled deep fryer to 375°F (190°C).

When oil is ready, add one-third to one-half of potato slices and cook in batches until golden and crisp, about 2 to 3 minutes. If using a pan, you may have to turn some of the chips for even browning using a set of heatproof tongs. Let oil reheat for a few minutes between batches.

Cook parsnip slices using the same method as for potatoes—they will cook in about half the time, shrink to a very small size, and turn a dark golden colour.

Cook the beet slices last. Fry them for 3 to 4 minutes, or until completely crisp and a dark red/brown colour. Slices will shrink to about half their original size. Drain well.

Seasoning the chips

In a large bowl, mix half the chips with 2 tablespoons (30 mL) Parmesan cheese and ¼ teaspoon (1 mL) pepper; toss to coat well. Add the rest of the chips and mix in remaining cheese and pepper.

Party Pretzels

A great bar snack for a party, or something to snack on during the game!

¾ tsp (4 mL) grated coarse sea salt, preferably fleur de sel

½ tsp (2 mL) freshly ground pepper

½ tsp (2 mL) dried dillweed

¼ tsp (1 mL) onion powder

⅛ tsp (0.5 mL) garlic granules or powder

1½ tsp (7 mL) finely minced lemon zest

6 cups (1.5 L) low-sodium pretzels, such as Safeway Eating Right brand

2 Tbsp (30 mL) olive oil

Makes 6 cups (1.5 L).
Per 1 cup (250 mL): 195 cals, 5.5 g fat, 0.6 g sat. fat, 506 mg sodium, 32.4 g carbs, 4 g protein

Beverage Suggestion: crisp, dry white wine, such as Sauvignon Blanc or Fumé Blanc; citrus-flavoured soda

In a small bowl, mix seasonings together, and then add lemon zest; mix well. In a large bowl, combine pretzels with oil; stir well to coat evenly. Stir seasoning mixture into pretzels gradually, tossing well to distribute evenly.

Store in an airtight container for up to 7 days.

Homemade Potato Chips

These chips always disappear rapidly—there are never any leftovers! Add a dip if desired but plain works too. This recipe requires a Japanese hand-held slicer (or a mandoline) to get the potato slices thin enough. You also need clean, lint-free tea towels for drying the potato slices.

Slice unpeeled potatoes $\frac{1}{32}$ inch (0.5 to 1 mm) thick, or as thin as possible. Soak slices in a large bowl of cold water for 10 to 15 minutes to remove starch. Drain slices and rinse with cold water. Spread out on a clean tea towel to dry and cover with a second towel to absorb water. Dry slices by gently lifting up the towels and lightly tossing; the goal is to completely dry the potato slices before frying.

Line a heatproof pan with paper towels for draining chips after frying. Preheat the deep fryer, or fill a large, deep skillet with oil not more than one-third full. (If your skillet is 4 inches [10 cm] deep, fill it with 1 inch [2.5 cm] oil.)

Heat oil to 375°F (190°C), about 5 minutes on medium-high, until rippling but not smoking. If oil is ready, a test slice of potato should bubble up and cook to golden in 45 to 60 seconds. Fry chips in several batches; don't overcrowd them. Drain on the paper-towel-lined tray.

Transfer cooked chips to a large bowl and sprinkle with about ¼ teaspoon (1 mL) coarse ground salt; toss with tongs. Repeat salting and toss again to coat well.

2 medium red potatoes (about 6 oz [175 g] each), scrubbed

2 to 3 cups (500 to 750 mL) canola oil for deep-frying, or correct amount for your deep fryer

½ tsp (2 mL) coarse sea salt, preferably fleur de sel, or rock salt in a salt grinder

Serves 4.

Per serving: 197 cals, 13.7 g fat, 1 g sat. fat, 300 mg sodium, 16.3 g carbs, 1.9 g protein

Beverage Suggestion:
soda flavoured with lemon, lime, or cola; light beer

Cooking Tip: Add some freshly ground pepper with each toss if desired.

Seasoned Popcorn

Makes great flavoured snacks for family or friends; low carb, low cal, and economical!

Chili Lime

In a small saucepan, melt butter on low heat with all the ingredients except the popcorn and ⅛ teaspoon (0.5 mL) salt. Slowly pour seasoned butter over popcorn while stirring with a spoon to coat it well. Sprinkle popcorn with ⅛ teaspoon (0.5 mL) salt.

Peppered Parmesan

In a small saucepan, melt butter over low heat. Pour butter slowly over popcorn while stirring with a spoon, to coat it well. Sprinkle popcorn with salt and pepper, while stirring with a spoon to coat it well. Add cheese in the same way and stir well. Serve immediately.

Chili Lime

¼ cup (60 mL) butter, roughly chopped
1 Tbsp (15 mL) lime juice
¼ tsp (1 mL) Worcestershire sauce
1 tsp (5 mL) chili powder
¼ tsp (2 mL) salt
¼ tsp (2 mL) pepper
7 cups (1.75 L) popped popcorn, in a medium-large bowl
⅛ tsp (0.5 mL) salt

Makes 7 cups (1.75 L).
Per 1 cup (250 mL): 81 cals, 8.6 g fat, 4.2 g sat. fat, 18 mg cholesterol, 133 mg sodium, 0.6 g carbs, 0.1 g protein

Peppered Parmesan

¼ cup (60 mL) butter, roughly chopped
¼ tsp plus ⅛ tsp (3 mL) freshly ground pepper
¼ tsp (2 mL) salt
2 Tbsp (30 mL) finely grated Parmesan cheese
7 cups (1.75 L) popped popcorn, in a medium-large bowl

Makes 7 cups (1.75 L).
Per 1 cup (250 mL): 86 cals, 9 g fat, 4.5 g sat. fat, 19 mg cholesterol, 118 mg sodium, 0.3 g carbs, 0.8 g protein

Beverage Suggestion:
Mexican or light beer

Cooking Popcorn

In a medium-large 4-quart (4 L) pot, with a lid, place canola or corn oil and 3 or 4 "test kernels" of popcorn. Turn the heat to medium-high and preheat the oil, covered, until test kernels pop.

Add popcorn kernels and swirl the pot to coat the kernels with oil. Cover with the lid and cook on medium-high until popcorn starts to pop profusely; turn the heat down to medium. Shake the pot at times to move kernels around during cooking. Cook popcorn until popping subsides somewhat and then turn off the heat completely. Leave the pan on the stove for another 1 to 2 minutes so popping finishes, and then empty immediately into a medium-large bowl.

Cooking Tip: I recommend Orville Redenbacher's brand for popcorn because of its quality and consistency.

3 Tbsp (45 mL) canola or corn oil

½ cup (125 mL) popcorn kernels

Makes 14 cups (3.5 L) if kernels all pop.
(To cook 7 cups [1.75L] popcorn, use ¼ cup [60 mL] popcorn and 1.5 Tbsp [22.5 mL] oil.)

Per cup (250 mL): 55 cals, 3 g fat, 1 g sat. fat, 97 mg sodium, 6 g carbs 1 g protein

Black Bean Dip with Chips

An easy choice if you have a food processor; super-healthy, tasty, and it's vegan!

19 oz (560 mL) can black beans, rinsed and drained

1 Tbsp (15 mL) lime juice

1 tsp (5 mL) minced or puréed garlic

1 Tbsp (30 mL) chili powder

½ tsp (5 mL) ground cumin

¾ tsp (4 mL) salt

½ tsp (5 mL) ground black pepper

¼ tsp (1 mL) cayenne pepper

¼ cup (60 mL) green onions (about 2 or 3), trimmed and sliced thin

1 Tbsp (15 mL) fresh cilantro leaves, finely minced

salted tortilla chips for serving

Makes 2 cups (500 mL).
Per ¼ cup (60 mL) (without chips): 73 cals, 0.5 g fat, 0.1 g sat. fat, 230 mg sodium, 13 g carbs, 4.6 g protein

Beverage Suggestion:
lime margarita

In a food processor with a standard blade, blend beans, lime juice, garlic, and dry seasonings together until smooth, about 1 to 2 minutes. Scrape down the sides of the bowl with a spatula; blend again for 1 to 2 minutes more.

Transfer mixture to a medium bowl; stir in green onions and cilantro. Cover and refrigerate dip for several hours so flavours have a chance to infuse; remove from the fridge 30 minutes prior to serving. Serve dip with tortilla chips on the side.

Chili Con Queso Dip
with Tortilla Chips

Literally meaning "chili with cheese," it makes an addictive dip for tortilla chips but is equally good on Mexican Eggs Benedict (p. 15).

In a medium non-stick saucepan, heat cream with Velveeta cubes on medium-low, stirring frequently to incorporate melting cheese. Add other ingredients once cheese is fully melted. Serve warm with tortilla chips or veggies.

Cooking Tip: If you are substituting medium salsa for hot salsa, add ¾ teaspoon (4 mL) cayenne pepper. You can freeze this dip in an airtight container for up to 2 months. Thaw before serving and heat on low to melt cheese.

2 cups (500 mL) light cream (15 to 18% MF)

2 lb (1 kg) Kraft Velveeta cheese, cubed

1¾ cups (435 mL) hot, chunky purchased salsa

½ tsp (2 mL) salt

½ tsp (2 mL) minced garlic

1 Tbsp (15 mL) fresh cilantro
leaves, finely minced

tortilla chips or cut raw vegetables for serving

Makes 4 cups (1 L).

Per ¼ cup (60 mL) (without chips or veggies):
208 cals, 14 g fat, 9.5 g sat. fat,
42 mg cholesterol, 1126 mg sodium,
8.7 g carbs, 11.7 g protein

Beverage Suggestion:
Mexican or light beer; citrus soda

Tex Mex Tortilla Chips with Fresh Salsa

These chips are delicious and have a flaky, pastry-like texture when made with fried flour tortillas.

ten 8-inch (20 cm) flour tortillas
1 to 2 cups (250 to 500 mL) canola oil for deep-frying
1 recipe Mexican Seasoning (p. 127)
1 recipe Fresh Salsa (p. 127)

Makes 80 chips.
Per chip (without salsa): 21 cals, 1 g fat, 0.1 g sat. fat, 65 mg sodium, 2.6 g carbs, 0.4 g protein

Beverage Suggestion: pale ale or lager beer

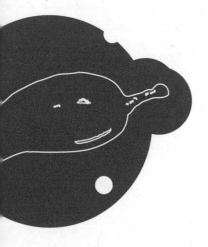

Cut each tortilla into 8 wedges and place back in the package (or in a plastic bag) to prevent from drying out. Pour ¾ inch (2 cm) oil into a large, deep frying pan and heat on medium-high. Be careful that depth of oil is no more than one-quarter the pan's total depth; do not overfill as oil will bubble up when chips are fried. Have a set of heatproof tongs ready and line a large baking dish with paper towels for draining chips. Place chip seasoning in a large bowl for tossing.

When oil is rippling but not smoking, add 8 to 10 tortilla wedges to the pan, spacing them out well so they do not overlap. Fry for about 30 seconds, and then check undersides for browning. When they are golden, flip them, and brown the other side for 30 to 60 seconds.

Transfer cooked chips to the paper-towel-lined tray to drain, and then quickly toss them into the spice mix. Seasoned chips can be moved to a plate or tray to cool completely. Repeat cooking, draining, and seasoning until all chips are cooked. Serve with salsa on the side.

Mexican Seasoning

If you are making this recipe to season Tex Mex Tortilla Chips (p. 126), mix the seasonings directly in the large tossing bowl.

Mix all ingredients together in a small bowl. Seasoning can be made ahead and stored in an airtight container for up to 3 months.

Seasoning

1 tsp (5 mL) garlic salt

1 Tbsp (15 mL) chili powder

¼ tsp (1 mL) cayenne pepper

¼ tsp (1 mL) ground black pepper

1 tsp (5 mL) ground cumin

½ tsp (2 mL) crushed oregano leaves

Makes 2 Tbsp (30 mL).

Per 2 Tbsp (30 mL): 59 cals, 2.4 g fat, 0.3 g sat. fat, 2441 mg sodium, 7.5 g carbs, 2 g protein

Fresh Salsa

This recipe is best made on the day it is to be used (hence the name "fresh salsa"), but you can prepare it a few hours ahead.
Dice tomato into ½-inch (1 cm) pieces and add to a medium bowl. Add all the other ingredients and mix well. Marinate, covered, in the fridge for at least 1 hour or up to 8 hours.

Salsa

2 large Roma tomatoes, quartered and seeds removed

⅓ medium sweet onion, diced

2 tsp (10 mL) minced jalapeno (about ½ a medium one)

1 Tsp (5 mL) lime juice

1 tsp (5 mL) sugar

½ tsp (2 mL) salt

¼ tsp (1 mL) pepper

1 Tbsp (15 mL) minced fresh cilantro leaves

Makes 1½ cups (375 mL).

Per Tbsp (15 mL): 4 cals, 50 mg sodium, 0.9 g carbs, 0.1 g protein

Salami Chips with Cream Cheese Dip

Guys love these chips! They are also very unique and super-easy to prepare.

3 inches (8 cm) of 4-inch (10 cm) diameter Genoa salami (preferably presliced into 36 pieces)
parchment paper for baking sheets

Makes 36 chips.
Per chip: 14 cals, 1.1 g fat, 0.4 g sat. fat, 4 mg cholesterol, 59 mg sodium, 0.1 g carbs, 0.8 g protein

Beverage Suggestion: medium-dark or full-bodied beer

Preheat the oven to 325°F (160°C) and line two large baking sheets with parchment paper. Ready any wooden spoons and rolling pins you own for shaping chips after baking. Position oven racks in the top third and bottom third of the oven.

If using unsliced meat, slice salami thinly into 36 rounds and lay pieces on baking sheets, positioned so they do not overlap.

Bake for 6 minutes, then turn each pan 180° for even baking. Bake for 6 minutes more, then remove from oven.

With a lifter, pick up each salami slice and curve it over a spoon handle or rolling pin. Cooling slices in this way shapes slices to look like chips; they will crisp up as they cool.

Cooking Tip: Ask the deli staff to precut your salami very thin, or use the smallest setting on a hand-held Japanese slicer (or mandoline) to do the same at home.

Cream Cheese Dip

A perfect dip for any chip! Try adding a tablespoon (15 mL) of your favourite fresh herb (finely chopped) such as basil, cilantro, or dill.

In a medium bowl, whisk together cream cheese and sour cream until smooth. Stir in seasoning and then add the green onion; mix well. You can make the dip to this point ahead of time; cover and refrigerate for up to 3 days. Remove from fridge 30 minutes before serving to soften.

8 oz (250 g) block regular or light cream cheese, at room temperature

½ cup (125 mL) regular or light sour cream

¾ tsp (4 mL) garlic salt

½ tsp (2 mL) pepper

¼ cup (60 mL) finely chopped green onions (about 3 medium trimmed ones)

Makes 1½ cups (375 mL).

Per Tbsp (15 mL) made with regular cream cheese: 45 cals, 4.3 g fat, 2.7 g sat. fat, 12 mg cholesterol, 92 mg sodium, 0.6 g carbs, 0.9 g protein

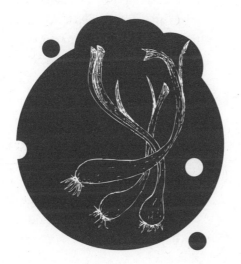

Wonton Crisps with Sweet and Sour Dipping Sauce

A light, crispy way to start an Asian-style meal, or serve as a terrific appetizer!

Dipping Sauce

2 tsp (10 mL) cornstarch

2 Tbsp (30 mL) rice or white vinegar

2 Tbsp (30 mL) sugar

½ cup (125 mL) chicken or vegetable stock

¼ cup (60 mL) ketchup

1 tsp (5 mL) sesame oil

½ tsp (2 mL) salt

¼ tsp (1 mL) ground Szechuan pepper

½ tsp (2 mL) Chinese chili-garlic sauce

1 Tbsp (15 mL) minced ginger

2 Tbsp (30 mL) finely chopped green onion (about 1)

Wonton Crisps

65 wonton wrappers (about half of a 1 lb [500 g] package)

1 to 2 cups (250 to 500 mL) canola oil for deep-frying, or correct amount for your deep fryer

Makes about 120 crisps, which serves 8.

Per 15 crisps with 2½ Tbsp (52.5 mL) dipping sauce: 143 cals, 5.2 g fat, 0.7 g sat. fat, 16 mg cholesterol, 386 mg sodium, 20.6 g carbs, 3.4 g protein

Beverage Suggestion:
crisp, dry white wine, such as White Zinfandel

Dipping Sauce

In a small saucepan, stir cornstarch into vinegar to dissolve it.

Add sugar, stock, ketchup, oil, and seasoning; mix well. Cook on medium heat, stirring constantly, until thickened slightly. Cool, cover, and refrigerate until needed or for up to 3 days. Reheat dipping sauce on low to serve with chips.

Wonton Crisps

Line a baking pan or baking sheet with paper towels for draining crisps after frying. Separate wonton wrappers from each other, and then use a sharp knife to cut them in half diagonally, making triangular pieces. Pile in a neat stack to cut several pieces at a time.

In a large, deep saucepan, or a pre-filled deep fryer, heat oil to 375°F (190°C) until rippling but not smoking. If using a saucepan, do not fill the pan any more than one-third full with oil.

Fry wrappers until golden and crisp, about 1 to 2 minutes. If wrappers are not totally submerged in oil, flip halfway through cooking using metal tongs or a strainer spoon to ensure an even golden colour. Drain well on the paper-towel-lined tray. Serve warm with dipping sauce on the side.

Fresh Vegetables with Lemon Feta Dip

Veggies and dip are essential for entertaining families and friends because they are well liked by all age groups and work for most people with special dietary requirements or preferences. Using regular (e.g. full fat) products in this dip will produce a richer, creamier dip but reduced fat or light products still make a tasty, enjoyable dip. The vegetables can be any ones you like to serve with dip; I have included a few of my favourites.

Starting with ¼ cup (60 mL) of the feta cheese, place all dip ingredients except chives in a small food processor and blend on medium-high for about 1 minute or until well incorporated. Or use a medium bowl and crush the feta with a soup spoon before whisking in the other dip ingredients until well blended.

Stir in the remaining ¼ cup (60 mL) feta cheese and the chives. Cover and refrigerate for at least 2 hours to allow the flavours to blend and the dip to thicken up. Dip can be made up to 2 days ahead; cover and refrigerate until serving.

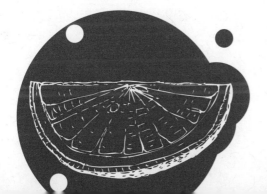

Lemon Feta Dip

½ cup (125 mL) feta cheese, crumbled or grated, divided

½ cup (125 mL) regular or light sour cream

¼ cup (60 mL) regular or calorie-reduced mayonnaise

1 Tbsp (15 mL) lemon juice

½ tsp (2 mL) cracked black pepper

¼ tsp (1 mL) onion salt

⅛ tsp (0.5 mL) garlic granules or ¼ tsp (1 mL) minced fresh garlic

2 Tbsp (30 mL) chopped fresh chives, or substitute finely chopped green onion

Vegetables

1 medium red, yellow, or orange bell pepper, cored, seeded, and cut into ½-inch (1 cm) strips

½ an English cucumber, sliced ¼ inch (6 mm) thick

1 Belgian endive, bottom ½ inch (1 cm) trimmed off and discarded, separated into leaves

1 pint (500 mL) basket cherry tomatoes, stems removed and discarded

Makes 1½ cups (375 mL).

Per ¼ cup (60 mL) full-fat dip and 1 cup (250 mL) veggies: 242 cals, 20.5 g fat, 5.7 g sat. fat, 26 mg cholesterol, 400 mg sodium, 10 g carbs, 4.5 g protein

Beverage Suggestion: Sauvignon Blanc

Sweet Treats

134 Bourbon Butter Tarts

135 Caramel Cookie Crisp

136 Sticky Toffee Pudding

138 Grand Marnier Ice Cream

139 Cherry Chocolate Killer Cobbler

140 Chocolate Caramel Filled Brownies

142 Kahlua Fudge Ice Cream Pie

143 Chocolate and Peanut
    Cookie Sandwiches

144 Classic Chocolate Chunk Cookies

145 Mrs. Knight's Ginger Snaps

146 Oatmeal Raisin Cookies

147 Hot Rods

148 New York Cheesecake with
    Fresh Strawberry Sauce

150 Mexican Chocolate Mousse

151 Chocolate Walnut Fudge

152 Lemon Meringue Pie

154 Lemon and Cream Pie

155 Molten Mocha Cakes

Bourbon Butter Tarts

Rich, buttery, and a family favourite; you can freeze these crowd pleasers if you hide them well!

30 unsweetened 3-inch (8 cm) tart shells, thawed if frozen

5 large eggs

1 cup (250 mL) brown sugar

¾ cup (185 mL) light or white corn syrup

2 tsp (10 mL) vanilla

1 Tbsp (15 mL) bourbon

⅓ cup (80 mL) melted butter

2 cups (500 mL) golden raisins

Makes 30 tarts.

Per tart: 247 cals, 10.9 g fat, 3.6 g sat. fat, 41 mg cholesterol, 194 mg sodium, 35.2 g carbs, 2.4 g protein

Beverage Suggestion: coffee or tea

Place racks in the top third and bottom third of the oven. Preheat the oven to 375°F (190°C). Place tart shells at least 1 inch (2.5 cm) apart on 2 large, rimmed baking sheets.

In a large bowl, beat eggs and sugar together with a whisk. Add corn syrup, vanilla, bourbon, and melted butter; mix well until smooth. Divide raisins among tart shells, about 1 tablespoon (15 mL) per shell. Spoon filling over raisins, distributing it equally; tart shells will be almost full.

Bake tarts for 25 minutes; rotating the pans halfway through baking. Let tarts cool to room temperature before serving.

Cooking Tip: Dark rum can be substituted for bourbon with excellent results.

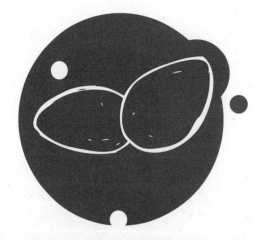

Caramel Cookie Crisp

Caramel apples with a chocolate-chunk cookie crust—the ultimate comfort dessert!!! Top with sweetened whipped cream or vanilla ice cream. Make 8 individual crisps by filling 3-inch (8 cm) ramekins; bake at 375°F (190°C) for 30 to 40 minutes on a tray to catch the drips.

Filling

Preheat the oven to 350°F (180°F) and oil a 1½ to 2 quart (1.5 to 2 litre) baking dish. Add lemon juice to a large bowl. Peel, quarter, core, and slice apples and pears ¼ inch (6 mm) thick, then cut slices in half lengthwise to make bite-size pieces. Add fruit to the bowl and toss with the lemon juice to prevent browning.

Add Kahlua to the fruit; mix well with a wooden spoon. In a medium bowl, mix dry ingredients together, then add to the fruit. Stir with the wooden spoon until dry ingredients are mixed in thoroughly—a brown syrup will result. Add this mixture to the baking dish; press down gently to distribute fruit into the corners and level the top.

Topping

In a medium, deep bowl, mix butter with brown sugar, flour, and cinnamon. Add oats, nuts, and chocolate; mix well until you have a crumbly dough (similar to cookie dough). Distribute mixture overtop fruit, covering it completely.

Bake for 60 minutes. Check to see if fruit is cooked through by poking it with a skewer to see if it is tender. If reheating, test fruit for tenderness after 30 minutes. Crisp will remain warm for 1 to 2 hours after baking but can also be reheated before serving. To reheat, place in a preheated 250°F (120°C) oven for 15 minutes.

Filling

3 Tbsp (45 mL) lemon juice

4 large Granny Smith apples

2 large Bartlett pears

2 Tbsp (30 mL) Kahlua liqueur

¾ cup (185 mL) white sugar

¼ cup (60 mL) brown sugar

3 Tbsp (45 mL) cornstarch

1 tsp (5 mL) cinnamon

vegetable oil for baking dish

Chocolate Chunk Topping

⅓ cup (80 mL) butter, at room temperature

¼ cup (60 mL) brown sugar

½ cup (125 mL) flour

1 tsp (5 mL) cinnamon

½ cup (125 mL) large-flake oats

¾ cup (185 mL) toasted walnuts or hazelnuts, coarsely chopped

2 oz (60 g) semi-sweet chocolate, chopped into ¼-inch (6 mm) chunks

Makes 8 servings.

Per serving: 463 cals, 18 g fat, 6.7 g sat. fat, 21 mg cholesterol, 8 mg sodium, 70.7 g carbs, 4.7 g protein

Beverage Suggestion: coffee or tea

Sticky Toffee Pudding

An English classic that has become a big favourite in North America too! Do not substitute all-purpose flour in this recipe; if necessary, make your own self-rising flour as per my instructions.

Pudding

Pudding

Preheat the oven to 350°F (180°C) and oil an 11 × 7 × 2 inch (28 × 18 × 5 cm) deep non-stick baking pan.

In a medium-small saucepan, bring dates and 1 cup (250 mL) water to a boil on medium-high heat. Reduce the heat to medium and simmer dates until tender, about 5 minutes. Remove from heat and cool for 5 minutes. Add baking soda; mix well with a wooden spoon. The mixture will foam and change colour—this is normal. Cool completely.

Using a hand-held mixer, or a stand mixer with a paddle attachment, cream butter with sugar in a large bowl until fluffy and pale yellow in colour, about 4 to 5 minutes. Add eggs one at a time, beating well after each addition; mix in vanilla. If using a hand-held mixer, switch to using a wooden spoon and mix in flour until just combined. If using a stand mixer, mix in flour on lowest speed. Stir in dates along with any liquid in the saucepan—the batter will look sloppy.

Pour batter into prepared pan and bake for 35 to 40 minutes, or until pudding is set and top springs slightly when pressed.

Pudding

vegetable oil or non-stick spray oil for pan

1 cup (250 mL) Medjool dates (about 6 oz [175 g]), pitted, chopped, and lightly packed

1 tsp (5 mL) baking soda

¾ cup plus 2 Tbsp (215 mL) golden or yellow sugar

2 large eggs

1 tsp (5 mL) vanilla

1¼ cups plus 1 Tbsp (325 mL) self-rising flour, sifted

Makes 8 servings.

Per serving: 347 cals, 19.6 g fat, 11.6 g sat. fat, 103 mg cholesterol, 414 mg sodium, 38.6 g carbs, 4.1 g protein

Beverage Suggestion: tea

Sauce

In a medium saucepan, melt butter with honey and sugar on medium heat, stirring frequently to dissolve the sugar. Bring to a boil and cook for 2 minutes more. Add cream and liquor. Remove from heat and stir until smooth.

Pour sauce overtop portions of warm pudding, using about 3 tablespoons (45 mL) per portion.

Making self-rising flour: In a medium bowl, measure out 1 cup minus 2 teaspoons (240 mL) all-purpose flour. Add 1½ teaspoons (7.5 mL) baking powder and ½ teaspoon (2 mL) salt; mix well with a spoon. Double or triple the ingredients for the amount of self-rising flour needed.

Makes 1 cup (250 mL).

To make enough for this recipe: Mix 1½ cups minus 1 tablespoon (360 mL) all-purpose flour with 2¼ tsp (11 mL) baking powder and ¾ tsp (4 mL) salt; mix well. Measure out 1¼ cups plus 1 Tbsp (325 mL) self-rising flour required for the Sticky Toffee Pudding recipe.

You will have about 3 tablespoons (45 mL) left over. Store the remaining mixture in an airtight container for future use.

Sauce

½ cup (125 mL) butter, at room temperature

¼ cup (60 mL) honey

½ cup (125 mL) packed dark brown sugar

¼ cup (60 mL) light cream (15 to 18% MF)

2 tsp (10 mL) dark rum, bourbon, or brandy

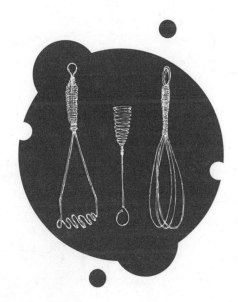

Grand Marnier Ice Cream

Super-easy and way too good! Crispy biscuits or wafers go well with this rich and creamy dessert. Sprinkle with cinnamon or cocoa for a different twist.

5 egg yolks from large eggs
½ cup plus 1 Tbsp (140 mL) sugar
1⅔ cups (410 mL) whipping cream
3 Tbsp (45 mL) Grand Marnier liqueur

Makes 6 servings.
Per serving: 393 cals, 31 g fat, 16.8 g sat. fat, 410 g cholesterol, 35 mg sodium, 23.2 g carbs, 5.5 g protein

Beverage Suggestion:
coffee; coffee cocktail, such as Monte Cristo (Kahlua and Grand Marnier)

Chill six 3-inch ramekins or a 1½ to 2 quart (1.5 to 2 litre) freezer-proof baking dish.

In a large bowl, whisk egg yolks with sugar until very pale and thick. The mixture should fall in ribbons when you lift out the whisk or spoon. Whisk in the liqueur. In the bowl of a stand mixer with a whisk attachment, or in a food processor, beat whipping cream on medium-high speed until soft peaks form. Scrape down the sides to incorporate any whipping cream clinging to the bowl; continue to beat on medium until stiff peaks form. Do not overbeat or cream will separate. Gently but thoroughly fold whipped cream into liqueur mixture. Divide evenly among the ramekins or fill the baking dish; level the top. Cover and freeze for 2 hours if using ramekins, or 4 hours (or overnight) for a large pan.

Cherry Chocolate Killer Cobbler

This is extremely rich, decadent, and over the top! Top servings with vanilla ice cream or whipped cream, if desired. You can use regular brandy for this recipe, or try cherry- or orange-flavoured brandy. Both fresh and frozen cherries will work but thaw frozen ones first.

Cherry Filling

In a small bowl, whisk sugar with cornstarch. In a medium saucepan, heat cherries and juice with brandy and lemon juice on medium. Add sugar/starch mixture; stir well to dissolve. Increase the heat to medium-high and bring the mixture to a boil, stirring constantly until mixture thickens, about 5 minutes. Let cool, stirring occasionally to prevent a skin from forming. Lightly oil six 3-inch ramekins and divide filling among them; cover and refrigerate.

Brownie Topping

Preheat the oven to 350°F (180°C). In a medium bowl, sift cocoa and whisk together with sugar. Stir in melted butter and vanilla; mix well. Beat in egg. Stir in flour and chocolate chips only until just combined; do not overmix. Place small clumps of brownie batter atop each ramekin, about ¼ cup (60 mL) per serving, and gently spread overtop cherry filling.

Bake cobblers for 25 minutes on the second rack from the top of the oven. Desserts can cool at room temperature for up to several hours before serving and can be reheated for 10 minutes at 300°F (150°C).

Cherry Filling

⅔ cup (160 mL) sugar

1 Tbsp plus 2 tsp (25 mL) cornstarch

2½ cups (625 mL) pitted, unsweetened dark red cherries with juice

1 Tbsp (15 mL) brandy

2 tsp (10 mL) lemon juice

vegetable oil for ramekins

Brownie Topping

⅓ cup plus 1 Tbsp (95 mL) dark Dutch cocoa powder

⅔ cup (160 mL) sugar

¼ cup plus 1 Tbsp (75 mL) melted butter

¼ tsp (1 mL) vanilla

1 large egg

3 Tbsp (45 mL) flour

½ cup (125 mL) chocolate chips

Serves 6 very lucky people.

Per serving: 489 cals, 17.1 g fat, 10.2 g sat. fat, 61 mg cholesterol, 13 mg sodium, 79.2 g carbs, 4.6 g protein

Beverage Suggestion:
robust, dry red wine, such as
Syrah, Bordeaux, or Malbec; Port

Chocolate Caramel Filled Brownies

Decadently delicious and finger-licking good!

Brownies

Brownies

½ cup (125 mL) butter

5 oz (150 g) unsweetened chocolate, finely chopped

3 large eggs

¾ cup (185 mL) white sugar

1 cup (250 mL) brown sugar

2 tsp (10 mL) vanilla

1¼ cups (310 mL) flour

1 Tbsp (15 mL) vegetable oil

¾ cup (185 mL) pecans, chopped and toasted

vegetable oil or non-stick spray oil for pan

Caramel Filling

25 caramels, preferably Kraft brand, wrappers removed

1 Tbsp (15 mL) whipping cream

Makes 40 pieces.

Per piece: 165 cals, 8.9 g fat, 4.4 g sat. fat, 25 mg cholesterol, 20 mg sodium, 19.5 g carbs, 1.6 g protein

Beverage Suggestion: cappuccino, coffee, or tea; ice cold milk

Preheat the oven to 350°F (180°C) and oil two 10-inch (25 cm) square cake pans. Line both pans with parchment paper, pressing it into the corners so oil adheres it to the sides of the pans.

In a medium saucepan, melt butter on low heat; add chocolate and stir to melt. Remove from heat to cool.

In a medium-large bowl, beat eggs, sugars, and vanilla until foamy and mixed well. Using a wooden spoon, stir in chocolate mixture until incorporated. Gradually add flour, stirring just until combined. Add oil and nuts; mix until just incorporated.

Divide batter between the prepared pans and spread evenly into the corners; level with a knife. Bake for 25 minutes, rotating pans halfway through the baking period. Cool completely in the pans, then remove one brownie layer but leave the other in its pan. If preparing layers ahead, wrap in plastic wrap and refrigerate to speed up the filling process.

Caramel Filling

In a medium saucepan, melt caramels with whipping cream, stirring frequently until caramels are thoroughly melted and mixture is smooth. Pour overtop brownie layer still in the pan and spread out evenly to coat entire surface. After removing parchment paper, place second brownie layer atop caramel filling. Seal the pan with plastic wrap and chill until filling is set—this step may take 60 to 90 minutes.

Ganache Icing

In a small saucepan, bring whipping cream to a boil on medium heat; add chocolate, cover, and remove from heat. Let sit for 5 minutes, and then stir until chocolate is entirely melted and mixture is smooth. Cool until thick enough to spread—not too runny. Spread icing evenly overtop caramel-filled brownie and chill until set, about 30 minutes in the fridge.

Cut pan into 5 equal rows along one side and 8 rows along the other to make 40 pieces about 1¼ × 2 inches (3 × 5 cm).

Ganache Icing
5 oz (150 g) chocolate chips
¼ cup (60 mL) whipping cream

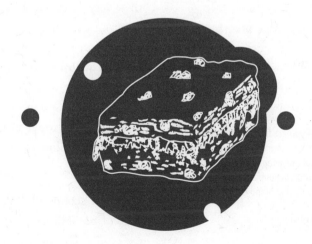

Kahlua Fudge Ice Cream Pie

A sensational dessert for a casual party! Start this recipe the day before so you have adequate freezing time.

Chocolate Crust

1½ cups (375 mL) chocolate cookie crumbs

3 Tbsp (45 mL) sugar

¼ cup (60 mL) melted butter

Filling

3 qt (3 L) vanilla ice cream

⅓ cup (80 mL) Kahlua liqueur

5 oz (150 mL) chocolate syrup, preferably Hershey's brand, divided

½ cup (125 mL) pecan halves, toasted

Serves 12 lucky people.

Per serving: 311 cals, 15.7 g fat, 7.3 g sat. fat, 36 mg cholesterol, 137 mg sodium, 38.7 g carbs, 3.7 g protein

Beverage Suggestion: coffee or mocha latte

Cooking Tip: If you are finishing this dessert the day before serving, cover the top loosely but completely with plastic wrap to keep the sauce and ice cream from drying out in the freezer For the best results, use Kahlua brand coffee liqueur.

Chocolate Crust

Preheat the oven to 375°F (190°C). In a medium bowl, stir together cookie crumbs and sugar; add melted butter and mix until crumbs are moist. Press firmly and evenly into a 10-inch (25 cm) deep-dish pie pan. Crust should be ¼ inch (6 mm) thick to reach all the way up the sides of the pan. Pack crumbs in tight to help the crust stay intact when serving.

Bake for 8 minutes. Cool completely; cover and chill in the freezer for 30 minutes before filling.

Filling

In a very large bowl, soften ice cream at room temperature for 15 minutes; break it into pieces with a wooden spoon. Add Kahlua and mix well until ice cream is smooth but still thick. Fill pie crust half full with ice cream. Drop tablespoonfuls (5 mL) of chocolate syrup over ice cream in shell, using two-thirds to three-quarters of total amount. Spoon more ice cream overtop chocolate syrup until shell is filled to top of crust. Cover and freeze pie for 8 hours. Freeze remaining Kahlua ice cream in a deep, narrow, covered container.

Assembly

Form 12 scoops of Kahlua ice cream and place around outside edge of pie. Fill in middle with additional scoops using up all the ice cream. Drizzle remaining chocolate syrup around top of pie. Sprinkle scoops with pecans and return pie to the freezer until 5 to 8 minutes before cutting and serving.

Chocolate and Peanut Cookie Sandwiches

Doubly delicious with two cookies, peanuts, and chocolate in the middle!

Preheat the oven to 400°F (200°C) and line 2 baking sheets with parchment paper, trimmed to fit. Smooth parchment to ensure cookies will bake flat.

In a medium bowl, whisk together egg white and icing sugar, then stir in melted butter. Using the whisk, stir flour and cocoa into egg-white mixture until smooth. Spoon 1½-teaspoon (7.5 mL) portion of batter onto the parchment-lined baking tray and spread out with a knife or the back of a spoon to make a 2½-inch (6 cm) circle. Repeat with remaining batter, spacing cookies at least 1½ inches (4 cm) apart; you should get 16 cookies.

Bake for 4½ to 5 minutes, until cookies are flat and batter is set. Cool completely, then peel off parchment paper. Turn 8 cookies over and return to baking sheet—they will be the bottom halves of the cookie "sandwiches." Reduce the oven temperature to 350°F (180°C).

Top each base with 2 tablespoons (30 mL) chocolate chips and sprinkle with 2 to 3 teaspoons (10 to 15 mL) chopped peanuts. Return pan to the oven for 3 minutes to melt the chocolate. Check to see if chocolate chips are melted by touching the top of a chip with your fingertip—heat for 1 to 2 minutes longer if chocolate is not melted. Remove from the oven and immediately top each cookie with a second cookie, aligning the edges to make a lid. Lightly press down on top to squeeze melted chocolate around peanuts and seal the sandwich together. Cool completely until chocolate firms up, about 20 to 30 minutes, or speed up this process by refrigerating for 10 to 15 minutes.

1 egg white, from a large egg

¼ cup plus 1 Tbsp (75 mL) icing sugar, sifted

2 Tbsp (30 mL) melted butter

3 Tbsp (45 mL) flour, sifted

1 Tbsp (15 mL) dark Dutch cocoa, sifted

1 cup (250 mL) chocolate chips

⅓ to ½ cup (80 to 125 mL) roasted peanuts, finely chopped

Makes 8 cookie sandwiches.

Per sandwich, made with 3 tsp (15 mL) peanuts: 277 cals, 15.5 g fat, 7.5 g sat. fat, 8 mg cholesterol, 16 mg sodium, 28.9 g carbs, 5.6 g protein

Beverage Suggestion: latte, coffee, or tea; ice cold milk

Cooking Tip: Instead of always using new pieces of parchment paper, you can purchase Silipat liners for your baking sheets; they are made of silicone and are good to 500°F (260°C). They are washable and reusable, and therefore more environmentally friendly.

Classic Chocolate Chunk Cookies

Voted most beloved cookie by North Americans!

¾ cup (185 mL) butter, at room temperature

1 cup (250 mL) brown sugar

1 tsp (5 mL) vanilla

1 large egg

1 tsp (5 mL) baking soda, sifted

1½ cups (375 mL) flour

6 oz (175 g) semi-sweet chocolate, chopped, or substitute 1 cup (250 mL) chocolate chips

vegetable oil for baking sheet

Makes 34 cookies.

Per cookie: 121 cals, 6.2 g fat, 3.7 g sat. fat, 17 mg cholesterol, 43 mg sodium, 15.2 g carbs, 1.3 g protein

Beverage Suggestion: coffee, mocha latte, or tea; ice cold milk

Preheat the oven to 375°F (190°C) and lightly oil 3 baking sheets.

In a large bowl, cream together butter and brown sugar with a wooden spoon, or use a stand mixer with the paddle attachment, or a hand-held mixer on medium speed. Beat in vanilla and egg until smooth. Add baking soda and flour; mix well by hand or on low speed. Stir in the chocolate.

Place 2-tablespoon (30 mL) portions of cookie dough onto prepared baking sheets, pressing into 2-inch (10 cm) circles. Space cookies about 2 inches (5 cm) apart. Bake for 10 to 12 minutes or until firm and golden brown. Cool on racks.

Cooking Tip: If you only have one baking sheet, wipe it with a paper towel to get rid of any loose cookie crumbs between rounds

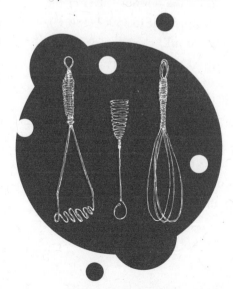

Mrs. Knight's Ginger Snaps

This recipe is from a lady who lived next door to my family when I was about three years old; she made these cookies for our family on a regular basis. They were our favourite! We also enjoyed her singing budgie birds and how her husband would flood his garden space in the winter for us to ice skate on.

Preheat the oven to 350°F (180°C) and lightly oil 2 baking sheets.

In a large bowl, cream butter with brown sugar with a wooden spoon until light and fluffy. Add molasses and beaten egg; beat well until thoroughly incorporated. Sift together the dry ingredients, then add them gradually to the butter mixture, mixing well with the spoon.

Portion out pieces of dough the size of a walnut, or about 1½ tablespoons (22.5 mL) per cookie, and form them into balls with your hands. Roll in white sugar to coat well and place on cookie sheets, spaced at least 2 inches (5 cm) apart. Lightly press down on tops until cookies are about ¼ inch (6 mm) thick. Bake for 8 to 10 minutes, or until they spring back when lightly touched.

Cooking Tip: If you prefer cookies that are chewy in the middle, bake them for 8 minutes at most. If you like cookies that snap or crunch, bake them for 10 minutes. If you are baking both trays of cookies at the same time, switch and turn the trays halfway through baking.

vegetable oil or spray oil for baking sheets

¾ cup (185 mL) butter, at room temperature

1 cup (250 mL) brown sugar

¼ cup (60 mL) molasses

1 large egg, beaten in a small bowl

2 cups (500 mL) flour

¼ tsp (1 mL) salt

2 tsp (10 mL) baking soda

1 tsp (5 mL) ground cinnamon

1 tsp (5 mL) ground ginger

1 tsp (5 mL) ground cloves

½ to ¾ cup (125 to 185 mL) white sugar in a small bowl for coating cookies prior to baking

Makes 36 cookies.

Per cookie: 92 cals, 4 g fat, 2.4 g sat. fat, 16 mg cholesterol, 92 mg sodium, 12.9 g carbs, 0.9 g protein

Beverage Suggestion:
ice cold milk

Oatmeal Raisin Cookies

The cinnamon adds a little pizzazz to these tasty morsels. Make sure you don't overcook them or they won't be chewy in the middle!

1 tsp (5 mL) baking soda, sifted
½ tsp (2 mL) cinnamon
¼ tsp (1 mL) salt
1 cup (250 mL) large-flake oats
1 cup (250 mL) flour
½ cup (125 mL) butter, at room temperature
1 cup (250 mL) brown sugar
1 large egg
½ tsp (2 mL) vanilla
¾ cup raisins (seedless sultanas, Thompson raisins, or golden raisins)

Makes 32 cookies.

Per cookie: 104 cals, 3.4 g fat, 1.9 g sat. fat, 15 mg cholesterol, 63 mg sodium, 17 g carbs, 1.6 g protein

Beverage Suggestion:
coffee, black tea, or chai tea; ice cold milk

Preheat the oven to 350°F (180°C) and lightly oil 3 baking sheets.

In a medium bowl, mix together first 5 ingredients. In a large bowl, cream together butter and brown sugar. Add egg and vanilla; beat until smooth. Gradually add dry ingredients, stirring well to combine. Stir in raisins.

Place 2-tablespoon (30 mL) portions of cookie dough onto prepared baking sheets and press them out to make 2-inch (5 cm) circles about ½ inch (1 cm) thick. Space cookies 2 inches (5 cm) apart.

Bake for 12 to 15 minutes, or until the cookies spring back when pressed lightly with a fingertip. Don't overcook; they should be chewy in the centre.

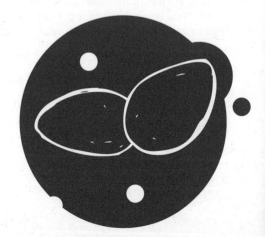

Hot Rods

I am not sure where the name came from, but they are a sweet treat from my childhood that satisfies my desire for coconut with dark chocolate! Double the recipe for serious cravings. See Ingredient Reference List (p. 157) for information on trans-fat-free shortening.

Lightly oil a large baking sheet or line it with parchment paper.

In a medium-large saucepan, whisk together sugar with cocoa until blended; add milk and stir with the whisk until mixture is smooth. Place the saucepan on medium-low heat and stir constantly until sugar is melted, about 5 minutes.

Turn the heat to medium and bring to a boil. When mixture is fully boiling, add shortening, oats, and salt; stir constantly and cook for 1 minute. Remove from heat and immediately add coconut and vanilla; mix well. Place 2-tablespoon (30 mL) portions of batter onto the baking sheet. Let stand for 30 minutes to harden before moving or serving.

vegetable oil, non-stick spray oil, or parchment paper for baking sheet

¾ cup (185 mL) sugar

3 Tbsp (45 mL) dark Dutch cocoa, sifted

¼ cup (60 mL) milk

¼ cup (60 mL) vegetable shortening, chopped and at room temperature

1½ cups (375 mL) large-flake oats

⅛ tsp (0.5 mL) salt

¾ cup (185 mL) unsweetened medium shredded coconut

1 tsp (5 mL) vanilla

Makes 22 treats.

Per treat: 103 cals, 4 g fat, 2.5 g sat. fat, 6 mg cholesterol, 14 mg sodium, 14.5 g carbs, 2 g protein

Beverage Suggestion:
hot chocolate or ice cold milk

New York Cheesecake with Fresh Strawberry Sauce

The ultimate cheesecake—not too sweet with a tangy sour cream topping and fresh strawberries! It is very rich and but it does serve 12. You will need a 9- or 10-inch (23 or 25 cm) springform pan that is 3 inches (8 cm) deep.

Chocolate Cookie Crust

1 cup (250 mL) chocolate cookie crumbs

2 Tbsp (30 mL) sugar

2 Tbsp (30 mL) melted butter

Cheesecake Batter

4 eggs, at room temperature

1¼ cups (310 mL) sugar

2 lb (1 kg) regular cream cheese

1 Tbsp (15 mL) lemon juice

1½ tsp (7.5 mL) vanilla

Makes 12 servings.

Per serving: 591 cals, 39.4 g fat, 23.7 g sat. fat, 175 mg cholesterol, 318 mg sodium, 49.5 g carbs, 9.8 g protein

Beverage Suggestion:
light, dry bubbly, such as Cordon Negro Brut, sparkling wine, or berry-flavoured soda

Preheat the oven to 350°F (180°C).

In a medium bowl, mix cookie crumbs with sugar. Add melted butter and mix well. Press mixture into the springform pan, packing it in tightly to cover the base. This way the crust will stay together better when cut and be easier to serve. Bake crust for 7 minutes then cool in pan on a rack.

Reduce the oven temperature to 325°F (160°C). Using a stand mixer with a paddle attachment or a hand-held mixer, beat eggs with sugar in a large bowl until well mixed.

Remove wrappers from cream cheese and place blocks on a microwavable plate. Heat on low or 40% power for 2 minutes, then check their softness. Repeat procedure for 1-minute intervals until all the cream cheese is very soft. Remove blocks as they soften up and add them to the egg mixture while continuing to heat the rest. This step will take about 5 to 8 minutes; the softer the cheese, the easier it is to beat and get a smooth batter.

Once you have added the last block of cream cheese, beat well until smooth. Beat on high for 2 minutes. Scrape down sides and bottom of bowl to incorporate any lumps. Repeat beating and scraping until batter is smooth. Add lemon juice and vanilla; beat on medium until well incorporated. Pour batter overtop crust. Bake cake for 1 hour. Cool for 15 minutes while you prepare the topping.

Increase the oven temperature to 350°F (180°C).

In a small bowl, mix sour cream with sugar and vanilla; keep refrigerated until ready to use. After cake has cooled for 15 minutes, spread with sweetened sour cream and smooth the top.

Bake for 7 minutes. Cool for 30 minutes in the pan on a rack, then refrigerate cake (still in the pan), uncovered, for several hours. Cover the pan and continue to refrigerate, at least overnight but preferably for 24 hours.

When ready to serve, run a knife around outer edge of cake to loosen filling from the sides of the pan. Release springform side handle and carefully remove outer ring from the pan. Smooth sides of cake with a palette or dinner knife.

Fill a 2-cup (500 mL) measuring cup with hot water. Soak a medium kitchen knife in the hot water for 1 minute to warm it, then remove and wipe dry with a clean cloth. If you cut each slice of cheesecake with a clean, heated knife, you will get smooth, attractive slices. Otherwise the cream cheese sticks to the knife and the pieces are jagged and a lot of cake is wasted. (See tip for advice on portioning the cake.) Top each slice with ¼ cup (60 mL) Fresh Strawberry Sauce.

Topping

2 cups (500 mL) regular sour cream

¼ cup (60 mL) sugar

1 tsp (5 mL) vanilla

1 recipe Strawberry Sauce (p. 10) for serving

Portioning cake into servings: For 12 pieces, cut the cake in half down the middle. Cut each of the 2 halves in two to create 4 quarters. Finally, cut each quarter into 3 pieces. If you don't need all 12 servings but want to portion the cake evenly, score the top of the cake as mentioned above, cut deep enough so you can see the cut lines clearly but don't cut completely through; cut and serve only the portions needed.

Mexican Chocolate Mousse

Easy and delicious! Try it as a cake filling or in a parfait layered with berries.

6 oz (150 g) semi-sweet chocolate, chopped into ½-inch (1 cm) pieces

2 cups (500 mL) whipping cream, cold (from the fridge)

½ tsp (2 mL) ground cinnamon

½ tsp (2 mL) vanilla

Serves 6.

Per serving: 419 cals, 36.4 g fat, 22.4 g sat. fat, 104 mg cholesterol, 31 mg sodium, 20 g carbs, 2.7 g protein

Beverage Suggestion: robust red wine, such as Syrah; Port; latte or coffee

Using a double boiler over hot but not boiling water, melt chocolate on medium-low heat. Stir frequently until completely melted and smooth. You can also melt chocolate in the microwave, using a glass or ceramic dish, on medium-low heat or 40% power. Heat chocolate for 2 minutes, then stir to incorporate melted chocolate. Heat for 1 minute more and stir again. Repeat heating in 1-minute intervals until completely melted. Cool chocolate to room temperature.

In a medium-large, deep bowl, beat whipping cream, cinnamon, and vanilla until soft peaks form, using a hand-held mixer or a stand mixer with a whisk attachment. Scrape down the sides of the bowl and beat again for 1 minute, or until stiffer peaks form. Be careful not to overbeat.

With a whisk, stir one-third of melted chocolate into whipped cream until well mixed. Add remaining chocolate, gently folding it in with the whisk. Scrape whipping cream off the whisk and bottom of the bowl with a spatula at least once during the folding stage to incorporate all the chocolate.

Spoon mousse into individual dessert bowls or wine glasses. Cover and refrigerate until serving, up to 1 day ahead.

Chocolate Walnut Fudge

The easiest recipe for the creamiest fudge I have ever had and definitely my husband Doug's favourite!

Lightly oil an 8-inch (20 cm) square baking pan.

Using a double boiler over hot but not boiling water, melt chocolate with condensed milk on medium-low heat. Stir frequently until incorporated and thickened. Remove from heat, add vanilla and walnuts; mix well. Cool to room temperature, which will take up to 1 hour.

Pour cooled mixture into the prepared pan and spread it into the corners with a spatula or palette knife. Cover and chill for at least 4 hours or overnight.

Run a dinner knife around the edge of the pan. Cut fudge into 8 rows across and 8 rows down to make sixty-four 1-inch (2.5 cm) squares. Run the knife under each piece before removing. Keep fudge covered and refrigerated until serving.

vegetable oil or non-stick spray oil for baking pan

12 oz (375 g) semi-sweet chocolate, chopped, or substitute 2 cups (500 mL) chocolate chips

10 oz (300 mL) can sweetened condensed milk, preferably Eagle Brand

1 cup (250 mL) toasted walnut halves, coarsely chopped

½ tsp (2 mL) vanilla

Makes 64 pieces.

Per piece: 60 cals, 3.3 g fat, 1.3 g sat. fat, 2 mg cholesterol, 6 mg sodium, 7 g carbs, 1 g protein

Beverage Suggestion: coffee or tea; ice cold milk

Lemon Meringue Pie

A well-loved North American classic! It is on the menu of many diners and coffee shops; some of which have never taken it *off* the menu, especially in smaller towns. Other establishments are offering it as a new item because many chefs are revisiting comfort foods from the 1950s, '60s and '70s—and for good reason. Start this recipe early in the day so there is enough time to cool the pie slowly.

Lemon Pie Filling

In a medium-large saucepan, mix sugar with cornstarch and salt using a whisk. Gradually add 3 cups (750 mL) of very hot tap water, whisking to combine until all the dry ingredients are wet and mixture is smooth. Place the saucepan on medium heat and bring the contents to a boil. Stir frequently to dissolve sugar. Once mixture is boiling, cover and cook for 2 minutes.

Reduce heat to medium-low and pour half the mixture into the bowl with the egg yolks; whisk well to combine. Add remaining sugar mixture and mix well. Return mixture to saucepan and cook for 1 minute, whisking constantly. Do not allow to boil. Remove from heat and add butter, vanilla, lemon juice, and lemon zest; mix well. Pour filling into warm pie crust and smooth out the top with a knife or the back of a spoon. Set aside.

Meringue

Preheat the oven to 350°F (180°C). Using a stand mixer with a whisk attachment or a hand-held mixer, beat egg whites with cream of tartar and salt on high speed in a large, deep mixing bowl until soft peaks form, about 2 to 3 minutes. With the whisk or beaters running on high speed, gradually add sugar, 1 tablespoon (15 mL)

Lemon Pie Filling

1 cup (250 mL) sugar

½ cup (125 mL) cornstarch

¼ tsp (1 mL) salt

4 egg yolks, slightly beaten in a medium bowl (save whites for Meringue)

1 Tbsp (15 mL) butter, at room temperature

¼ tsp (1 mL) vanilla

½ cup (125 mL) lemon juice

1 Tbsp (15 mL) lemon zest or finely grated lemon rind

10-inch (25 cm) deep-dish pie crust, just baked and still hot

Meringue

6 egg whites, at room temperature

½ tsp (2 mL) cream of tartar

¼ tsp (1 mL) salt

¾ cup (185 mL) sugar

Serves 8.

Per serving: 412 cals, 13.8 g fat, 4.3 g sat. fat, 199 mg cholesterol, 371 mg sodium, 65.7 g carbs, 6.4 g protein

Beverage Suggestion: tea or coffee

at a time, sprinkling it at the outer edge of the bowl and being careful not to put the spoon or your hand anywhere near the moving whisk or beaters. Adding sugar this gradually usually takes about 10 minutes in total. If sugar builds up on outside edges of meringue; stop the mixer and scrape down the sides of the bowl with a spatula before continuing. Beat meringue until all sugar has been added and mixture is creamy, shiny, and has stiff peaks.

Assembly and Baking

Spread Meringue overtop Lemon Filling, covering entire top to the very edges where pastry starts since Meringue will shrink as it cooks. However, cooking the pie with the crust and filling still warm and cooling the pie gradually will reduce the overall shrinkage. Using a spatula or palette knife, pat all over top of Meringue, making up and down motions to form decorative peaks.

Bake pie in the middle of the oven for 15 minutes or until tips of Meringue peaks are golden. Cool pie on a rack for 2 hours, or until it reaches room temperature, then refrigerate, uncovered, until cold, about 2 hours.

Lemon and Cream Pie

This version is for those people who just do not like meringue or who find it a bit too sweet. Piled-high whipped cream is the obvious solution to that problem! Start this recipe really early in the day or, better yet, the day before so the pie crust is cooked and filling is set. If you chill the bowl and whisk before making the topping, your whipping cream will stiffen up faster than at room temperature.

10-inch (25 cm) deep-dish pie crust, baked and cooled

1 recipe Lemon Pie Filling (p. 152), cooled to room temperature

2 cups (500 mL) whipping cream, well chilled

⅓ cup (80 mL) icing sugar, sifted

¾ tsp (4 mL) vanilla

Serves 8.

Per serving: 549 cals, 34.8 g fat, 17.4 g sat. fat, 277 mg cholesterol, 285 mg sodium, 53.4 g carbs, 5.5 g protein

Beverage Suggestion: tea or coffee

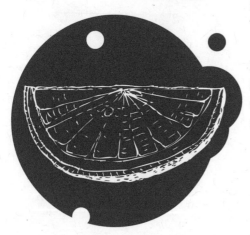

Pour Lemon Pie Filling into pie crust and refrigerate, uncovered, all day or overnight to set the filling.

Using a stand mixer with a whisk attachment or a hand-held mixer, beat whipping cream with sugar and vanilla in a large, deep bowl on medium-high until soft peaks start to form, about 4 to 5 minutes. Scrape down the sides of the bowl and stir to incorporate any remaining liquid. Continue beating on medium-high, watching carefully, for 1 to 2 minutes more, until stiff peaks form. If still not at this stage, beat for 10- to 15-second intervals until firm peaks form. Do not overbeat or cream will separate. You want the whipped cream to be firm so it holds its shape on top of the pie.

Spread whipped cream overtop filled pie, staying inside the pastry edge but covering Lemon Filling entirely. Using a spatula or palette knife, pat all over surface of whipped cream, making up and down motions to form decorative peaks. Refrigerate, uncovered, for up to 4 hours before serving.

Molten Mocha Cakes

Rich little wonders that can be prepared a day ahead and baked just before serving. You can also double this recipe without a problem.

Preheat the oven to 425°F (220°C) and generously butter four 6-ounce (185 mL) ramekins.

In a medium saucepan, melt butter on low heat with instant coffee; mix well with a spoon. Add chocolate and stir constantly until melted completely. Immediately remove from heat and let cool for 5 minutes.

In a large bowl, whisk 3 whole eggs, 3 egg yolks, and vanilla until frothy. (Reserve the 3 extra egg whites for another use, such as making meringue for Lemon Meringue Pie [p. 152], or freeze in an airtight container for up to 3 months.)

Gradually beat in icing sugar, mixing well until smooth. Stir in chocolate mixture using the whisk. Add flour and whisk until completely incorporated. Divide batter evenly among the 6 ramekins. The cakes can be made ahead to this point, covered, and refrigerated for up to 1½ days.

Bake cakes for 15 minutes, or 18 minutes if baking straight from the fridge. Let cool for 5 minutes; cakes should be puffy, firm around the edges, and soft and runny in the middle. Wearing oven mitts, run a table or palette knife around outside of each cake and then turn ramekins one by one onto serving plates. Tap the bottoms of the baking dishes so cakes fall out; if this fails to happen, run the knife around the edge again.

Serve warm with ¼ cup (125 mL) ice cream per person.

½ cup plus 2 Tbsp (155 mL) butter

1 tsp (5 mL) instant coffee granules (do not substitute finely ground coffee or espresso powder)

7 oz (200 g) semi-sweet chocolate, such as Lindt or Baker's, chopped

6 large eggs, divided

1 tsp (5 mL) vanilla

1½ cups (375 mL) icing sugar

½ cup (125 mL) flour

1 cup (250 mL) vanilla ice cream for serving

Serves 4.

Per serving: 927 cals, 56.2 g fat, 31.1 g sat. fat, 534 mg cholesterol, 78 mg sodium, 92.5 g carbs, 12.9 g protein

Beverage Suggestion:
coffee; coffee cocktail, such as Monte Cristo (Kahlua and Grand Marnier)

Ingredient Reference List and Recommended Brands

Bacon: I suggest natural bacon made without preservatives, such as Harvest brand thick slice, or bacon from a local butcher where they smoke it themselves.

Balsamic vinegar: The aged ones are the most expensive but taste the best. Pick one from a reputable company. Bargain brands can taste watery.

Brown sugar: Generally use dark brown, such as Best Brown, and not demerara.

Butter: Generally use unsalted, especially for desserts. If you substitute salted, you may want to cut back on any salt in the recipe.

Chili-garlic sauce: Use Chinese chili-garlic sauce or substitute sambal oelek and minced garlic. Asian Family brand is readily available.

Chocolate: Specified by sweetness, i.e., Baker's unsweetened, semi-sweet. I recommend Callebault, Lindt, or Ghirardelli.

Cocoa: Unsweetened dark Dutch cocoa powder, available in the bulk section or the baking aisle of most grocery stores. Many brands are not dark and produce products that are lighter in colour, flavour, and intensity.

Dijon mustard: Use Maille or another French brand for the best flavour.

Dry mustard: Also known as mustard powder and available in the spice section of grocery stores.

Eggs: Use large size, and preferably free-range ones, especially for omelettes and egg entrées.

Extracts: Flavourings, such as vanilla, almond, or orange, should be pure extracts for the best flavour.

Flour: All-purpose white (regular or unbleached) unless otherwise specified.

Golden sugar: A soft, lighter version of brown sugar. It has finer granules and gives cakes a light caramel taste and pale gold colour. The flavour is less intense than brown sugar. Pack it to measure as you would for brown sugar. Sometimes labelled as "yellow sugar."

Greek Seasoning: Available in the spice section of the grocery store. I recommend Krinos brand if you have a choice.

Hoisin sauce: Asian sauce base made from soybeans; available in the Asian section of the grocery store. Asian Family brand is readily available, in addition to many others.

Honey: Liquid honey, not solid, creamed, or crystallized honey.

Icing sugar: Also known as confectioner's sugar or powdered sugar.

Instant Asian noodles: Use 400-gram packages of Rooster or Diamond brand, available in the Asian section of most grocery stores. Each package will have 7 portions of compressed noodles.

Ketchup: Also known as catsup; I suggest Heinz brand for recipe flavour consistency.

Light cream or cereal cream: Use 15 to 18% milk fat cream.

Margarine: Block margarine may be substituted for butter if you have an allergy or dairy restriction, but the recipe may taste slightly different. Use canola- or corn-based products for the best flavour, not soybean. Be aware that hydrogenated margarines do contain trans fats. Earth Balance makes a vegan butter-flavoured stick margarine made from a combination of palm, soybean, canola, and olive oils, which has zero trans fats. It is tasty and bakes like butter or margarine. The same company also makes a shortening with the same combination of oils.

Mayonnaise: Use Kraft Real Mayonnaise or Hellmann's mayonnaise for the best flavour.

Milk: Whole or homogenized milk (5% milk fat); otherwise specified as canned, evaporated, etc.

Olive oil: Pomace olive oil is okay for frying but use extra virgin olive oil for dressings and drizzling.

Panko breadcrumbs: Japanese-style breadcrumbs with a light, crispy texture, which creates a golden crunchy coating when deep-fried. I suggest Kikkoman or Asian Family because these brands have few or no additives.

Pasta: I recommend purchasing dried Italian pasta made from semolina wheat only (no eggs added). I cook the pasta a bit longer than the manufacturers suggest; their instructions usually yield very *dente* pasta. Test for doneness to reach desired tenderness. Some good brands are La Molisana, Riscossa, or Delverde.

Prawns: 16/20 or 21/30 count per pound frozen raw prawns, tail-on or easy-peel are preferred.

Rice vinegar: Available in the Asian section of grocery stores, or substitute white vinegar.

Whole roasted red peppers: I recommend Tosca or Italissima brand. Available in jars in the condiment section of grocery stores. Sometimes they also stock julienne-sliced ones.

Semolina flour: Available in the flour section of large grocery stores and at Italian delis or import stores. I recommend La Molisana brand.

Sherry vinegar: Available at Italian and Spanish delis. Like fine cognac or wine, the price is determined by the number of years it has been aged; 30- to 50-year-old vinegar is far more expensive but far better tasting.

Shortening: Hydrogenated vegetable oil. Fluffo and Crisco are common brands but both contain trans fats. Earth Balance makes a solid shortening that works well for pastry and has no trans fats. The same company also makes a solid margarine that also has no trans fats.

Stocks: Regular fat-free chicken or beef as listed, unless specified as low-sodium, especially for recipes where the product will be boiled to reduce the volume. I use regular Pacific stock or Knorr brand. If I must purchase any other brands, I buy low-sodium types because they generally do not contain MSG.

Sugar: Granulated white from sugar beets or sugarcane unless another kind is specified.

Spices: Ground unless otherwise specified as whole, etc.

Tomatoes: For canned ones, use crushed, diced, or whole; "no name" brands are acceptable.

Tortillas: I suggest Olafson's brand flour tortillas for the best results and flavour. They are strong when heated (less breakage), fold easier, and taste great.

Yellow sugar: Use golden sugar or light brown sugar.

Whipping cream: 32% to 35 % milk fat cream.

Worcestershire sauce: Use a reputable brand, such as Heinz or HP, not a "no name" one. If you need a pure vegetarian product, without anchovy, then substitute a vegetarian "Worcestershire-style" sauce, which is available in health food stores.

Metric Conversion Chart

These measurements have been rounded off and are therefore not exact.
Use only as a guideline for easy calculations.

Volume Equivalents

1 tablespoon (Tbsp) = 3 teaspoons (tsp) = ½ fluid ounce (oz) = 15 millilitres (mL)

2 Tbsp = 6 tsp = 1 oz = 30 mL

¼ cup = 4 Tbsp = 2 oz = 60 mL

⅓ cup = 5 Tbsp plus 1 tsp = 2⅔ oz = 80 mL

½ cup = 8 Tbsp = 4 oz = 125 mL

⅔ cup = 10 Tbsp plus 2 tsp = 5⅓ oz = 160 mL

¾ cup = 12 Tbsp = 6 oz = 185 mL

1 cup = 16 Tbsp = 8 oz = 250 mL

1 pint = 2 cups = 16 oz = 500 mL

1 quart = 2 pints = 4 cups = 32 oz = 1000 mL or 1 litre (L)

1 gallon = 4 quarts = 8 pints = 16 cups = 128 oz = 4000 mL or 4 L

Weight Equivalents

½ pound (lb) = 8 oz = 250 grams (g)

1 lb = 16 oz = 500 g

1 kilogram (kg) = 1000 g = 2.2 lb

1 litre (L) = 1000 mL water = 1 kg

Standard Baking Pan Sizes and Capacity

medium loaf pan: 8½"× 4½"× 2½"; 6 cups

large loaf pan: 9"× 5"× 3"; 8 cups

medium rectangular pan: 11"× 7"× 2"; 8 cups

large rectangular pan: 13"× 9"× 2"; 12 cups

medium baking pan: 14½"× 10½"× 2"; 10 cups

large baking pan: 16¼"× 11¼"× 2"; 12 cups

medium square pan: 8"× 8"× 2"; 8 cups

large square pan: 9"× 9"× 2"; 10 cups

small round pan: 8"× 2"; 7 cups

medium round pan: 9"× 2"; 8 cups

deep medium pan: 9"× 3"; 12 cups

large round pan: 10"× 2"; 10 cups

medium springform pan: 9"× 2½"; 10 cups

large springform pan: 10"× 2¾"; 15 cups

medium baking sheet:10¼"× 15¼"

large baking sheet: 11"× 17"

individual pizza pan: 8" (20 cm)

medium-large round pizza pan: 12" (30 cm)

Index

A

Appetizers
  Also see Snacks
  Black Bean Dip, 124
  Blackened Scallops with Honey Lime
    Butter, 36
  Bruschetta, 37
  Cajun Calamari Rings, 73
  Chili Cheese Croquettes, 38
  Chili Con Queso Dip with Tortilla Chips, 125
  Coconut Prawns with Mango Sauce, 46
  Chorizo and Sweet Pepper Pizza, 70
  Corn and Cheese Fritters, 40
  Crab Stuffed Mushroom Caps, 39
  Curried Yam Fries with Cucumber Cilantro
    Dip, 57
  Damn Good Prawns, 41
  Grilled Chicken Quesadillas, 50
  Hot Halibut Sliders, 65
  Hot Italian Sausage Rolls with Honey Lemon
    Dijon Dip, 44
  Italian Meatball Sliders, 64
  Mardi Gras Grilled Prawns, 42
  Mexican Beef Dip with Tortilla Chips, 49
  Mushroom Crostini, 43
  Mussels with Lime Cilantro Sauce, 51
  Pissaladiere, 56
  Pork Tenderloin Nuggets, 72
  Power Crunch Chicken Wings with Spicy
    Barbecue Sauce, 80
  Salami Chips with Cream Cheese Dip, 128
  Salt and Pepper Chicken Wings, 82
  Salt and Pepper Cocktail Ribs, 82
  Taquitos with Guacamole Sauce, 52
  Tex-Mex Tortilla Chips with Fresh Salsa, 126
  Ultimate Popcorn Shrimp, 48
  Uncle Doug's Nachos, 83
  Vegetables with Lemon Feta Dip, 131
  Wonton Crisps with Sweet and Sour
    Dipping Sauce, 130
Apples
  Caramel Cookie Crisp, 135
Avocados
  Guacamole Sauce, 53

B

Bacon
  Bacon and Egg Salad with Dijon
    Vinaigrette, 22
  BLT Salad (bacon, lettuce, tomato), 24
  BGOT Grilled Cheese Sandwich (bacon,
    green onion and tomato), 26
  Breakfast Baguette Sandwiches, 6
  Mexican Eggs Benedict, 15
Baked Blueberry and Brie Bread Pudding, 12
Baked Eggs Ranchero Style, 13
Baked Penne with Bolognese Sauce, 88
Balsamic Beef Panini, 27
Balsamic Wine Sauce, 28
Banana
  Banana Chocolate Chip Pancakes, 9
Bar Brittle, 115
Barbecue, *see Grilled/Barbecued*
Beans
  Black Bean Dip, 124
  Stoplight Chili, 76

Beef/Veal
  Baked Penne with Bolognese Sauce, 88
  Balsamic Beef Panini, 27
  Candied Beef Tenderloin with Balsamic
    Butter, 101
  Cheddar Stuffed Beef Burgers, 63
  Italian Meatball Sliders, 64
  Meatball Panini, 80
  Mexican Beef Dip with Tortilla Chips, 49
  Mocha Chili Rubbed Steak, 102
  Prime Rib Roast with Red Wine Gravy, 109
  Taquitos with Guacamole Sauce, 152
  Texan Flank Steak, 96
Black Bean Dip, 124
Blackened Scallops with Honey Lime Butter, 26
Blueberries
  Baked Blueberry and Brie Bread Pudding, 12
  BGOT Grilled Cheese Sandwich (bacon, green
    onion, tomato), 26
  BLT Salad (bacon, lettuce, tomato) with Shallot
    Dressing, 24
Bourbon Butter Tarts, 134
Breads
  French Toast and Baked Breakfast Items,
    see Breakfast and Brunch
  Ham and Cheese Breakfast Buns, 5
  Honey Cinnamon Buns, 2
  Pizza and pizza dough, *see Pizza*
  Sandwiches, *see Sandwiches*
Breakfast Baguette Sandwiches, 6
Breakfast Burritos, 7
Breakfast and Brunch
  Baked Blueberry and Brie Bread Pudding, 12
  Baked Eggs Ranchero Style, 13

Banana Chocolate Chip Pancakes, 9
Breakfast Baguette Sandwiches, 6
Breakfast Burritos, 7
Ham and Cheese Breakfast Buns, 5
Heavenly Hash, 14
Honey Cinnamon Buns, 2
Mexican Eggs Benedict, 15
Strawberry Cream Waffles, 10
Sunshine French Toast, 8
Bruschetta, 37
Burgers
    Cheddar Stuffed Burgers, 63
    Hot Halibut Sliders, 65
    Italian Meatball Sliders, 64

C
Caesar Salad
    Cajun Caesar Salad, 20
    Chili Prawn Caesar Salad, 21
    Classic Caesar Salad, 18
Cajun Calamari Rings, 73
Cakes
    Molten Mocha Cakes, 155
    New York Cheesecake with Fresh Strawberry
        Sauce, 148
Candied Beef Tenderloin with Balsamic Butter,
    101
Candies/Confections
    Bar Brittle, 115
    Chocolate Walnut Fudge, 151
    Hot Rods, 147
Cheddar, *see Cheese*
Cheddar Stuffed Beef Burgers, 63

Cheese
    Baked Blueberry and Brie Bread Pudding, 12
    Baked Penne with Bolognese Sauce, 88
    BGOT Grilled Cheese Sandwich, 26
    Balsamic Beef Panini, 27
    Breakfast Baguette Sandwiches, 6
    Breakfast Burrito, 7
    Cheddar Stuffed Beef Burgers, 63
    Chili Cheese Croquettes, 38
    Chili Con Queso Dip with Tortilla Chips,
        125
    Chorizo and Sweet Pepper Pizza, 70
    Grilled Vegetable Panini, 29
    Ham and Cheese Breakfast Buns, 5
    Meatball Panini, 30
    Mexican Beef Dip with Tortilla Chips, 49
    Parmesan Veggie Chips, 118
    Pissaladière, 56
Cheesecake
    New York Cheesecake with Fresh Strawberry
        Sauce, 148
Cherry
    Cherry Chocolate Killer Cobbler, 139
Chicken
    Cajun Chicken Caesar Salad, 20
    Chicken with Jalapeno and Lime, 94
    Debbie Fried Chicken (DFC), 74
    Grilled Chicken Poutine, 62
    Grilled Chicken Quesadillas, 50
    Power Crunch Chicken Wings with Spicy
        Barbecue Sauce, 80
    Salt and Pepper Wings, 82
Chicken with Jalapeno and Lime, 94

Chili con Carne
    Chili Cheese Fries, 77
    Stoplight Chili, 76
Chili Cheese Croquettes, 38
Chili Cheese Fries, 77
Chili Con Queso Dip with Tortilla Chips, 125
Chips
    Salami Chips with Cream Cheese Dip, 128
    Homemade Potato Chips, 12
    Parmesan Veggie Chips, 118
    Tex-Mex Tortilla Chips with Fresh Salsa, 126
    Wonton Crisps with Sweet and Sour
        Dipping Sauce, 130
Chocolate
    Caramel Cookie Crisp, 135
    Cherry Chocolate Killer Cobbler, 139
    Chocolate and Peanut Cookie Sandwich, 143
    Chocolate Caramel Filled Brownies, 140
    Chocolate Walnut Fudge, 151
    Classic Chocolate Chunk Cookies, 144
    Hot Rods, 147
    Kahlua Fudge Pie, 142
    Mexican Chocolate Mousse, 150
    Molten Mocha Cakes, 155
Chorizo and Sweet Pepper Pizza, 70
Chowder, *see Soup*
Clams, *see Seafood and Fish*
Classic Spaghetti Carbonara, 91
Coconut Prawns with Mango Sauce, 46
Cookies
    Chocolate and Peanut Cookie Sandwiches,
        143
    Classic Chocolate Chunk Cookies, 144

Hot Rods, 147
Mrs. Knight's Ginger Snaps, 145
Oatmeal Raisin Cookie, 146
Corn
    Corn and Cheddar Fritters, 40
    Corn and Chili Chowder, 33
    Grilled Corn with Chili Lime Butter, 95
    Seasoned Popcorn, 122
Corn and Chili Chowder, 33
Cream Cheese Dip, 129
Creole Seasoning, 73
Cobblers/Crisps
    Caramel Cookie Crisp, 135
    Cherry Chocolate Killer Cobbler, 139
Cucumber Cilantro Dip, 57
Curried Cashews, 113
Curried Yam Fries, 57

D
Damn Good Prawns, 41
Debbie Fried Chicken (DFC), 74
Desserts and Sweets
    Bourbon Butter Tarts, 134
    Caramel Cookie Crisp, 135
    Cherry Chocolate Killer Cobbler, 139
    Chocolate Caramel Filled Brownies, 140
    Chocolate Walnut Fudge, 151
    Grand Marnier Ice Cream, 138
    Hot Rods, 147
    Kahlua Fudge Pie, 142
    Lemon and Cream Pie, 154
    Lemon Meringue Pie, 152
    Mexican Chocolate Mousse, 150
    Molten Mocha Cakes, 155

Mrs. Knight's Ginger Snaps, 145
New York Cheesecake with Fresh Strawberry
    Sauce, 148
Oatmeal Raisin Cookies, 146
Sticky Toffee Pudding, 136
Dips
    Chili Con Queso Dip with Tortilla Chips, 125
    Cream Cheese Dip, 129
    Cucumber Cilantro Dip, 57
    Guacamole, 53
    Honey Lemon Dijon Dip, 45
    Lemon Feta Dip, 131
    Mexican Beef Dip, 49
Double Fried French Fries, 58

E
Eggs
    Bacon and Egg Salad, 22
    Baked Blueberry and Brie Bread Pudding, 12
    Baked Eggs Ranchero Style, 13
    Breakfast Baguette Sandwiches, 6
    Breakfast Burritos, 7
    Heavenly Hash with Poached Eggs, 14
    Mexican Eggs Benedict, 15
    Quick Quiche, 16
    Sunshine French Toast, 8
Entrees, see Main Dishes

F
Fish, see Seafood and Fish
Fish and Chips, 108
Flank Steak
    Texan Flank Steak, 96
Fries
    Chili Cheese Fries, 77

Curried Yam Fries with Cucumber Cilantro
    Dip, 57
Double Fried French Fries, 58
Grilled Chicken Poutine, 62
Oven Fries, 61
Pomme Frites, 60
Fritters
    Corn and Cheddar Fritters, 40
    Zucchini Lace, 100
Fruit Desserts
    Caramel Cookie Crisp, 135
    Cherry Chocolate Killer Cobbler, 139
    Lemon and Cream Pie, 154
    Lemon Meringue pie, 152

G
Ginger Chicken Noodle Soup, 31
Ginger Garlic Ribs, 78
Grand Marnier Ice Cream, 138
Greek Pasta Salad, 25
Grilled/Barbecued
    Candied Beef Tenderloin with Balsamic
        Butter, 101
    Chicken with Jalapeno and Lime, 94
    Grilled Chicken Poutine, 62
    Grilled Chicken Quesadillas, 50
    Grilled Corn with Chili Lime Butter, 95
    Mocha Chili Rubbed Steak, 102
    Texan Flank Steak, 96
Guacamole Sauce, 53

H
Halibut
    Halibut au Gratin, 99
    Hot Halibut Sliders, 65

Heavenly Hash, 14
Herb Croutons, 19
Homemade Potato Chips, 121
Honey Lemon Dijon Dip, 45
Hot Halibut Sliders, 65
Hot Italian Sausage Rolls with Honey Lemon
    Dijon Dip, 44
Hot Potatoes, 104
Hot Rods, 147

I

Ice Cream Desserts
    Grand Marnier Ice Cream, 138
    Kahlua Fudge Pie, 142
Italian Meatball Sliders, 64

K

Kahlua Fudge Pie, 142

L

Lemon
    Lemon and Cream Pie, 154
    Lemon Meringue Pie, 152
Lime
    Chicken with Jalapeno and Lime, 94
Linguine, *see Pasta*

M

Macaroni, *see Pasta*
Main Dishes
    Baked Penne with Bolognese Sauce, 88
    Blackened Scallops with Honey Lime
        Butter, 36
    Candied Beef Tenderloin with Balsamic
        Butter, 101
    Cheddar Stuffed Beef Burgers, 63

    Chicken with Jalapeno and Lime, 94
    Chorizo and Sweet Pepper Pizza, 70
    Classic Spaghetti Carbonara, 91
    Coconut Prawns with Mango Sauce, 46
    Debbie Fried Chicken (DFC), 74
    Fish and Chips, 108
    Halibut au Gratin, 99
    Linguine with Red Clam Sauce, 90
    Mardi Gras Grilled Prawns, 42
    Mocha Chili–Rubbed Steaks, 102
    Pork Tenderloin Nuggets, 72
    Prime Rib Roast with Red Wine Gravy,
        109
    Spaghettini with Meatballs and Marinara
        Sauce, 86
    Stuffed Mac and Cheese, 92
    Tempura Fish with Lemon Caper Sauce,
        106
    Texan Flank Steak, 96
Mango Sauce, 47
Mardi Gras Grilled Prawns, 42
Marinara Sauce, 87
Marinades, *see Sauces/Marinades/Rubs/*
    Seasonings
Meatball Panini, 30
Mediterranean Vegetable Panini, 29
Mexican Beef Dip, 49
Mexican Chocolate Mousse, 150
Mexican Eggs Benedict, 15
Mocha Chili Rubbed Steak, 102
Molten Mocha Cakes, 155
Mrs. Knight's Ginger Snaps, 145
Mushrooms

Crab Stuffed Mushroom Caps, 39
    Mushroom Crostini, 43
    Stuffed Mac and Cheese, 92
Mussels, *see Seafood and Fish*

N

Nut mixes, *see Snacks*
Nuts and Bolts, 117

O

Onion Rings, 66
Oven Fries, 61

P

Parmesan Veggie Chips, 118
Party Pretzels, 120
Pasta
    Baked Penne with Bolognese Sauce, 88
    Classic Spaghetti Carbonara, 91
    Ginger Chicken Noodle Soup, 31
    Greek Pasta Salad, 25
    Linguine with Red Clam Sauce, 90
    Spaghettini with Meatballs and Marinara, 96
    Stuffed Mac and Cheese, 92
Pastries and Pies
    Bourbon Butter Tarts, 134
    Lemon and Cream Pie, 154
    Lemon Meringue Pie, 152
    Quick Quiche, 16
Pepper
    Peppered Pecans, 112
    Salt and Pepper Chicken Wings, 82
    Salt and Pepper Cocktail Ribs, 82
    Salt and Pepper Sesame Snacks, 116
Pies, *see Pastries and Pies*

Pizza
    Chorizo and Sweet Pepper Pizza, 70
    Pissaladière, 56
    Pizza Dough, 68
    Smoked Salmon Pizza, 71
Pomme Frites, 60
Potatoes, Sweet Potatoes, and Yams
    Curried Yam Fries, 57
    Double Fried French Fries, 58
    Grilled Chicken Poutine, 62
    Heavenly Hash, 14
    Homemade Potato Chips, 121
    Hot Potatoes, 104
    Manhattan Clam Chowder, 32
    Oven Fries, 61
    Pommes Frites, 60
    Potato Chip Gratin, 105
    Spicy Sausage and Red Potato Chowder, 34
    Warm Potato Salad, 98
    Zucchini Lace Fritters, 100
Potato Chip Gratin, 105
Pork
    Bacon and Egg Salad, 22
    BGOT Grilled Cheese Sandwich, 26
    BLT Salad with Shallot Dressing, 24
    Breakfast Baguette Sandwiches, 6
    Chorizo and Sweet Pepper Pizza, 70
    Classic Spaghetti Carbonara, 91
    Ginger Garlic Ribs, 78
    Hot Italian Sausage Rolls with Honey, Lemon Dijon Dip, 44
    Italian Meatball Sliders, 64
    Meatball Panini, 30

Pork Tenderloin Nuggets, 72
    Salami Chips with Cream Cheese Dip, 128
    Salt and Pepper Cocktail Ribs, 82
    Spicy Sausage and Red Potato Chowder, 34
Pork Tenderloin Nuggets, 72
Poultry, see Chicken
Power Crunch Chicken Wings with Spicy Barbecue Sauce, 80
Prawns, see Seafood and Fish
Puddings, Custards, and Mousse
    Baked Blueberry and Brie Bread Pudding, 12
    Grand Marnier Ice Cream, 138
    Mexican Chocolate Mousse, 150
    Sticky Toffee Pudding, 136

Q
Quick Quiche, 16

R
Red Hot Peanuts, 114
Rubs, see Sauces, Marinades, Rubs, and Seasonings

S
Salads
    Bacon and Egg Salad with Lemon Dijon Dressing, 22
    BLT Salad with Shallot Dressing, 24
    Cajun Chicken Caesar Salad, 20
    Chili Prawn Caesar Salad, 21
    Classic Caesar Salad, 18
    Greek Pasta Salad, 25
    Warm Potato Salad with Lemon Dijon Mayonnaise, 98
Salami Chips with Cream Cheese Dip, 128

Salt
    Salt and Pepper Cocktail Ribs, 82
    Salt and Pepper Sesame Snacks, 116
Sandwiches
    Balsamic Beef Panini, 27
    BGOT Grilled Cheese Sandwich, 26
    Breakfast Baguette Sandwiches, 6
    Meatball Panini, 30
    Mediterranean Vegetable Panini, 29
Sauces, Marinades, Rubs, and Seasonings
    Chili Con Queso Dip with Tortilla Chips, 125
    Creole Seasoning, 73
    Guacamole Sauce, 53
    Mango Sauce, 47
    Marinara Sauce, 87
    Mexican Seasoning, 127
    Mocha Chili Rub, 103
    Wine Gravy, 110
Scallops, see Seafood and Fish
Seafood and Fish
    Blackened Scallops with Honey Lime Butter, 36
    Cajun Calamari Rings, 73
    Chili Prawn Caesar Salad, 21
    Coconut Prawns with Mango Sauce, 46
    Crab Stuffed Mushroom Caps, 39
    Damn Good Prawns, 41
    Fish and Chips, 108
    Halibut au Gratin, 99
    Hot Halibut Sliders, 65
    Linguine with Red Clam Sauce, 90
    Manhattan Clam Chowder, 32

Mardi Gras Grilled Prawns, 42
Mussels with Lime Cilantro Sauce, 51
Quick Quiche, 16
Smoked Salmon Pizza, 71
Tempura Fish with Lemon Caper Sauce, 106
Ultimate Popcorn Shrimp, 48
Seasonings, *see Sauces, Marinades, Rubs, and Seasonings*
Seasoned Popcorn, 122
Shrimp, *see Seafood and Fish*
Snacks
Bar Brittle, 115
Chili Con Queso Dip with Tortilla Chips, 125
Curried Cashews, 113
Homemade Potato Chips, 121
Nuts and Bolts, 117
Parmesan Veggie Chips, 118
Party Pretzels, 120
Peppered Pecans, 112
Red Hot Peanuts, 114
Salt and Pepper Sesame Snacks, 116
Seasoned Popcorn, 122
Tex-Mex Tortilla Chips with Fresh Salsa, 126
Vegetables with Lemon Feta Dip, 131
Wonton Crisps with Sweet and Sour Dipping Sauce, 130
Soups
Corn and Chili Chowder, 33
Ginger Chicken Noodle Soup, 31
Manhattan Clam Chowder, 32
Spicy Sausage and Red Potato Chowder, 34
Spaghetti/Spaghettini, *see Pasta*

Spicy Sausage and Red Potato Chowder, 34
Squares and Bars
Chocolate Caramel Filled Brownies, 140
Salt and Pepper Sesame Snacks, 116
Steak, *see Beef*
Sticky Toffee Pudding, 136
Stoplight Chili, 76
Strawberry
New York Cheesecake with Fresh Strawberry Sauce, 148
Strawberry Cream Waffles, 10
Stuffed Mac and Cheese, 92
Sweet Potatoes, *see Potatoes, Sweet Potatoes, and Yams*

T
Taco Beef, 84
Taquitos with Guacamole Sauce, 52
Tarts, *see Pastries and Pies*
Tempura Fish with Lemon Caper Sauce, 106
Texan Flank Steak, 96
Tex-Mex Tortilla Chips with Fresh Salsa, 126

U
Ultimate Popcorn Shrimp, 48
Uncle Doug's Nachos, 83

V
Veal, *see Beef*
Vegetables
Curried Yam Fries, 57
Double Fried French Fries, 58
Grilled Corn with Chili Lime Butter, 95
Hot Potatoes, 104
Onion Rings, 66

Oven Fries, 61
Pomme Frites, 60
Potato Chip Gratin, 105
Warm Potato Salad, 98
Vegetables with Lemon Feta Dip, 131
Zucchini Lace Fritters, 100

W
Walnuts
Chocolate Walnut Fudge, 151
Warm Potato Salad, 98
Whipped Cream
Lemon and Cream Pie, 154
Strawberry Cream Waffles, 10
Wine Gravy, 110
Wonton Crisps with Sweet and Sour Dipping Sauce, 130

Y
Yams, *see Potatoes, Sweet Potatoes, and Yams*
Z
Zucchini Lace, 100

Acknowledgments

Thank you to the following people who helped make this book happen:

Ruth Linka, my publisher, for her continual support, patience, and knowledge. Her excitement and conviction about my first cookbook, *Go Nuts*, helped strengthen my confidence, and made it easy to jump into *Cravings*.

Holland Gidney, my editor, who got my concept for *Cravings* from the very beginning. I appreciate all her great ideas and creative details, especially with names and titles. Her patience and diligence helped me calmly walk down the writing path instead of stumbling and falling repeatedly.

Pete Kohut, designer, for his imagination, creativity, and genuine interest in this project. An additional thank you for all the recipe testing he did for *Go Nuts*.

Tara Saracuse for her enthusiasm, inventiveness, and persistence. I appreciated her constant help in promoting *Go Nuts*, and I look forward to working with Sheena to make *Cravings* a household word in every kitchen.

Everyone at TouchWood Editions who continues to support and encourage authors; you helped turn my writing experiences into positive, rewarding endeavours.

Dad and Irene for their continual love and encouragement.

Special thanks to Brenda, my sister, for her enthusiasm when *Go Nuts* was released and for her avid promotion of the same. Also, for being as excited about new recipes as I am.

Wayne, Laura, Joel, Logan, and Ashley for being my test kitchen audience and official tasters. I hope to expand this group to include Greg, Susan, Scott, and Dan on a regular basis when they make it out to the west coast.

My friend Scott Quinney for continually supporting culinary adventures (especially mine, of course) and actively participating in promoting *Go Nuts* (I hope you are interested in a second promotion).

Rob and Aurora for their love of good friends and fine food. Doug and I cherish your friendship and we always look forward to the fun and laughter that goes with getting together for dinner. Doug and I thank you both for your large purchase of *Go Nuts* cookbooks and your continual interest in *Cravings*.

Chris and Colin at Alchemy Hair Design and Anthony from Dolce Vita Coffee Art, both located in Victoria, BC, for their excitement and promotion of *Go Nuts*. Like Scott, I am crossing my fingers that you are ready and willing for another round with *Cravings*.

Go Nuts: Recipes that Really Shell Out
Debbie Harding

978-1-926741-11-6 • $19.95

Brie and Walnut Stuffed Figs
Pumpkin Pecan Pancakes
Honey Almond Spread

Just a few of the extraordinary nut-themed dishes from *Go Nuts*, the first cookbook to feature an all-nut cast of culinary delight.

Fish On: Seafood Dishes that Make a Splash
Ingrid Baier

978-1-926741-12-3 • $19.95

Tequila Lime Grilled Halibut
Tandoori Salmon with Mango Chutney
Crab Bisque

Just a few of the mouth-watering recipes from *Fish On*, a seafood lover's guide to the true tastes of the Pacific.